'This book is an excellent resource for occupational (and other) therapists and teachers working in an inclusive education setting. Providing evidence-based practical strategies for facilitating all children's early physical and cognitive development, the book will contribute greatly to the success of inclusion at the child, classroom and whole-school level. An excellent example of how occupational therapists can collaborate with teachers to develop a curriculum that enables children with special needs to participate optimally in mainstream school settings in the early years. Occupational therapists in both the UK and other contexts worldwide will find inspiration and practical strategies to develop a "client-centred, solution-focused, strength-based, occupation-based, collaborative, context-based, educationally-relevant and evidence-based" role in schools, as recommended in the World Federation of Occupational Therapists' Position Statement on Occupational Therapy Services in School-Based Practice for Children and Youth (2016). Highly recommended!'

Dr Debbie Kramer-Roy, Director Education of the European MSc in Occupational Therapy, Founding Member of the International School-Based Occupational Therapy (SBOT) Network and RCOT-SS-CYPF Clinical Forum on SBOT, and Prinicipal Investigator of the Collaborative Action Research project "Developing the Role of Occupational Therapy in Inclusive Education in Pakistan".

'Such a helpful book for early years and primary trainee teachers and busy educators! This excellent book offers a wealth of expertise that shows how children's physical development and cognition are interconnected. Written in a clear and accessible style, it offers lots of straightforward and practical ideas to help support our youngest learners in school.'

Karen Vincent, Senior Lecturer in Early Years and Primary Education, Canterbury Christ Church University

'This book is a "must have" for all early years' practitioners. It is highly practical and user-friendly, whilst also providing a very comprehensive resource designed to support professionals in the provision of effective strategies to promote early physical and cognitive development. The beautiful illustrations complement the evidence-based strategies proposed by the authors, whose combined expertise and experience in this area make this an absolutely invaluable resource for all. Highly recommended for all formal and informal early years settings.'

Dr Susana Castro-Kemp, Reader in Education, Roehampton University

'Written from the perspectives of a teacher and occupational therapist, this book brings together the best of both worlds in a very accessible and easy to digest way.

The straightforward strategies and activities to 'put you in the shoes' of the children will help readers to understand what is happening in the Early Years setting and what can be done to further promote learning and life skills of the whole class.'

*Dr Karina Dancza, Assistant Professor Occupational Therapy,
Health and Social Sciences Cluster, Singapore Institute of Technology.*

'This is such an excellent book for all SENCOs and teachers and I would highly recommend it. It is very informative and is broken down into clear sections so that specific information can be obtained easily. The authors strike an excellent balance between theory and practice making it very easy to read. Suggestions for future practice are sensible and achievable in a busy school environment. The passion they demonstrate for supporting both physical and cognitive development in the early years shines through in each section and is also very clear to see.'

*Karen Ward, Key Stage One mainstream teacher and SENCO,
The Lady Joanna Thornhill Primary School, Wye, Kent*

'This is a really excellent book that is packed with information. Each section provides sound professional advice.'

*Maria Elsam, Primary Science Team leader, Chartered Science Teacher,
Faculty of Education, Canterbury Christ Church University*

'For the busy SENCO this book is a very welcome "one-stop" guide to support the development of their own and their setting's practice.'

Leanne Bennett, SENCO, Sandwich Infants School.

Universal Approaches to Support Children's Physical and Cognitive Development in the Early Years

This book has been designed to provide educators with practical strategies and approaches to support the motor and coordination development of children within an educational setting. Difficulties with movement and coordination can significantly affect participation and learning, in Early Years settings and schools, but many of these children can be supported through changes to their educational environment, or the implementation of universal strategies.

This invaluable resource demonstrates how professionals can positively impact on children's educational progress, outcomes and social participation.

This book:

- Combines perspectives of occupational therapy and special educational needs, using evidence-based research to provide professionals with the knowledge and confidence to enhance quality first teaching skills for all children, in all settings.
- Promotes inclusion and participation in activities that affect pupil progress, such as handwriting, self-care, lunchtime, physical activities and play.
- Offers a range of activities, tips and guidance to help improve progress and academic achievement for all children.

Taking a holistic approach to early learning and teaching, this is a vital resource for teachers and trainee teachers, teaching assistants, SENCOs, student occupational therapists and all practitioners working in Early Years settings.

Sue Soan is a university lecturer, supervising doctoral students on research relating to special educational needs. She is also an educational adviser for fostering organisations and schools and undertakes clinical supervision with school leaders. Prior to 2003 Sue taught in nursery settings, primary mainstream and special schools for over 25 years, as a classroom teacher, a subject coordinator (mathematics), a special educational needs coordinator (SENCO) and Senior Leader. Her doctoral thesis (2013) explored the education provision of Looked after Children who had experienced early life abuse and neglect. Her research interests include the SENCO role, motor and coordination development, multi-professional working, Looked after Children, autism and clinical supervision. As an authority in her field, she has published in peer reviewed journals and presented her research at national and international conferences. Sue is a school governor at a mainstream primary school and is a Trustee of a national SEN organisation.

Eve Hutton started her career over 25 years ago as a children's occupational therapist in the National Health Service (NHS), supporting children with additional needs in Early Years and school settings. She was awarded a National Institute for Health Research (NIHR) scholarship, gaining a PhD in Health Services Research at the University of Kent in 2000. Subsequently, she pursed a career in Higher Education, most recently as a reader in Children's Health and Wellbeing at Canterbury Christ Church University. Her research interests include therapy provision in schools and the therapy support needs of parents of children with complex needs. As an authority in her field, she has published widely in peer reviewed journals and presented her research at national and international conferences. Eve is a school governor at a specialist school for children with profound, severe and complex learning difficulties.

Universal Approaches to Support Children's Physical and Cognitive Development in the Early Years

Sue Soan and Eve Hutton

LONDON AND NEW YORK

First published 2021
by Routledge
2 Park Square, Milton Park, Abingdon, Oxon OX14 4RN

and by Routledge
52 Vanderbilt Avenue, New York, NY 10017

Routledge is an imprint of the Taylor & Francis Group, an informa business

© 2021 Sue Soan and Eve Hutton

The right of Sue Soan and Eve Hutton to be identified as authors of this work has been asserted by them in accordance with sections 77 and 78 of the Copyright, Designs and Patents Act 1988.

All rights reserved. No part of this book may be reprinted or reproduced or utilised in any form or by any electronic, mechanical, or other means, now known or hereafter invented, including photocopying and recording, or in any information storage or retrieval system, without permission in writing from the publishers.

Trademark notice: Product or corporate names may be trademarks or registered trademarks, and are used only for identification and explanation without intent to infringe.

British Library Cataloguing-in-Publication Data
A catalogue record for this book is available from the British Library

Library of Congress Cataloging-in-Publication Data
Names: Soan, Sue, author. | Hutton, Eve, author.
Title: Universal approaches to support children's physical and cognitive development in the early years / Sue Soan and Eve Hutton.
Description: Abingdon, Oxon ; New York, NY: Routledge, 2021. | Includes bibliographical references and index.
Identifiers: LCCN 2020022389 (print) | LCCN 2020022390 (ebook) | ISBN 9780367541262 (hardback) | ISBN 9780367265212 (paperback) | ISBN 9780429293610 (ebook)
Subjects: LCSH: Child development. | Motor ability in children. | Cognition in children. | Early childhood special education.
Classification: LCC LB1115 .S69 2021 (print) | LCC LB1115 (ebook) | DDC 371.9/0472–dc23
LC record available at https://lccn.loc.gov/2020022389
LC ebook record available at https://lccn.loc.gov/2020022390

ISBN: 978-0-367-54126-2 (hbk)
ISBN: 978-0-367-26521-2 (pbk)
ISBN: 978-0-429-29361-0 (ebk)

Typeset in Univers
by Swales & Willis, Exeter, Devon, UK

Contents

Foreword ix
About the authors xi
Acknowledgements xiii
About this book xv

Introduction 1

Chapter 1 Physical skills, movement and learning 5

Chapter 2 Personal independence skills for learning and participation 17

Chapter 3 Are they sitting comfortably? 34

Chapter 4 Confident handwriting 44

Chapter 5 Working together with parents and carers – sign posting ideas for home 61

References and resources 68
Index 73

Foreword

The basis of this book originated from work undertaken by the authors over several years experimenting with the development of universal resources designed for use by teachers and those working in Early Years education. The combined perspectives of occupational therapy and special educational needs have been brought to bear on everyday issues and challenges affecting young children's development. The authors believe that these shared professional perspectives originating within health and education are important, especially in relation to young children and their learning.

The book aims to show that this kind of multidisciplinary knowledge can help children's educational progress, outcomes and social participation skills through greater awareness of the impact of the school and classroom environment, and greater understanding of children's movement and coordination development. In embarking on this quest we have encountered difficulties and barriers about professional language and terminology, professional boundaries and responsibilities, but our belief in this way of working has never faltered (Lewis 2019). Additionally, research has shown that parents of children with movement and coordination needs, such as dyspraxia, view educators' and health professionals' input as essential to help them support their child in the home as well as in the learning environment (Kehily 2013; Pedro *et al.* 2019).

The ideas were partly driven by work in schools that recognised the benefit of occupational therapists sharing their professional knowledge with educators (Hutton 2009a, 2009b). Therapists were able, in these settings, to meet the needs of children with complex needs and those with motor and coordination difficulties by developing whole school/group interventions, promoting learning and social participation.

This work took place within the context of an exponential rise in the numbers of children entering school who were 'not ready' (Steele *et al.* 2016; The Marmot Review 2010) and increases in the numbers of children with mild to moderate differences likely to affect their development and academic progress. We wanted to show that it was possible to encapsulate the knowledge used by occupational therapists and advice from SENCOs and to package this in a way that was accessible for educators and other adults to use in nurseries and schools. We trialled these resources with teachers and, based on feedback, developed them further and considered how they could be incorporated within a nursery or school environment (Hutton and Soan 2010, 2015). We considered questions such as:

- How much support do nursery nurses and teachers need when implementing these types of interventions?
- Who is best placed in the nursery/school to work with in terms of introducing new ideas?
- Is it possible to build on existing initiatives already available widely in schools to help facilitate the uptake of resources?

It is the culmination of this work that we present in this book. It is hoped that the information, strategies, approaches and evidence-based research offered in the book will provide Early Years and primary school educators, school nurses, occupational therapists and all trainees with the knowledge and confidence to enhance quality first teaching skills for all children, in all settings. Its aim is to broaden the knowledge base of educators and other appropriate practitioners with regards to the importance of promoting inclusion and participation in activities that affect pupil progress, including handwriting, self-care tasks such as managing lunchtime, and participation in physical activities and play.

It is anticipated that by implementing the guidance in this book practitioners will see how this approach to early movement and coordination development will:

- help improve progress and academic achievement for all children;
- help develop self-confidence and social participation for children with motor and coordination needs;
- develop practitioner confidence in supporting the motor and coordination difficulties of children within an educational setting;
- embed a holistic approach to early learning and teaching, recognising the links between physical, social and communication, and cognitive development within the generic curriculum;
- support an integrated approach to Continuing Professional Development across professional boundaries; and
- provide parents with an understanding of the importance of motor and coordination development on children's academic progress.

Finally, it is hoped that the suggestions provided in this book will help to further and enhance inclusive practice.

About the authors

As you will read in the following paragraphs, both authors' experience as practitioners has led them to conclude that children develop holistically. From an occupational therapy perspective, that a child's participation and engagement in meaningful activity enable them to develop independence and self-determination, and from an educator's point of view, that all developmental domains influence the others and thus impact on a child's cognition, physical, sensory, and social and emotional wellbeing. We also think that the environment is important in determining how children develop in their early years. Indeed, we strongly believe that early experiences at nursery and school contribute to lifelong levels of motivation, participation and engagement in learning.

Sue Soan – *the teacher*

Working as a special needs teacher in the 1990s with children eager to learn but failing to make progress, Sue acknowledged their frustrations and disappointments and started searching for answers. She took time to ask the children what they found hard to do, to observe when they had difficulties and how they were constrained in the classrooms. Sue saw how the children's movement, coordination and sensory development impacted on every aspect of their school day. Reflecting on her own limited knowledge, training and understanding about how the physical development of the child (including visual, auditory and oral) impacted on learning, she contacted health colleagues, such as Occupational Therapists (OT), Optometrists (O) and Speech and Language Therapists (SALT), to help her develop programmes of work that merged all aspects of a child's development in harmony. The outcomes for the children were outstanding – academically, physically, socially and emotionally – and since this time she has never doubted the value and positive contribution of professionals from different disciplines working together for the benefit of a child.

Eve Hutton – *the occupational therapist*

By the time children start their Early Years education they are expected to have mastered basic skills enabling them to participate and learn at school. They need to be able to take off their coat in the morning, go to the toilet independently, eat lunch, play with other children, sit and attend in the classroom and hold a pencil. As a children's occupational therapist, Eve's role was to help children who, through disability or delay, struggled with functional skills. Observing children in Early Years and school settings, Eve realised that many children, not only those referred for occupational therapy, had difficulty with these skills. Eve realised that by working closely with teaching staff and parents, solutions that worked for individuals could be adapted and scaled up for the benefit of all children. Eve has worked throughout her career as an occupational therapist, in the National Health Service and Higher Education, promoting universal and whole class/school approaches in schools.

Together

Thus, it seemed essential to write this book together, breaking down the barriers between professions whilst still providing expert knowledge about the development of children and the daily experiences of the practitioner in classroom environments.

Dr Sue Soan (Educator) and Dr Eve Hutton (Occupational Therapist)

Acknowledgements

The authors would like to offer their sincere thanks to Bill Hutton for his excellent illustrations, which have been essential to the production of this book. Also, thanks to the family who provided the images.

We acknowledge the contribution that Lesley Perry (OT) and Marian Nairac (OT) made, as part of the 'OT into Schools' project in 2008, to ideas and ways of working in schools. The 'OT into Schools' project was completed whilst Marian and Lesley worked for Kent Community Health Foundation NHS Trust.

We would also like to thank John McParland (Principal), Sarah Lacon (Vice Principal) and Hatice Ahmet (Primary SENCO) from The John Wallis Academy for providing the case study in Chapter 4.

Finally, we would like to thank all the many individuals, colleagues, children and families who have helped us in schools, and elsewhere, to undertake our research.

About this book

The basis of this book originated from work undertaken by the authors and developed collaboratively, over several years experimenting with the development of resources designed to be utilised by teachers in their daily practice (Hutton and Soan 2010). The ideas were partly driven by the acknowledgement that occupational therapists could demonstrate their ability not only to meet the needs of individual children with complex difficulties, but also by working with whole class approaches potentially benefiting a greater number of children at risk of coordination or movement issues. This was in the context of an exponential rise in the numbers of children entering school who were 'not ready' (Steele *et al.* 2016) and increases in the numbers of children with mild to moderate difficulties likely to affect their development and academic progress. We wanted to show that it was possible to encapsulate the knowledge of occupational therapists and Special Educational Needs Coordinators (SENCOs) and package them in a way that was accessible for educators and other adults to use in nurseries and schools. We trialled these resources with teachers and based on their feedback developed them further in order to produce this book.

It is therefore hoped that this book will provide Early Years and primary school educators, school nurses, occupational therapists and all trainees, with practical strategies, approaches and evidence-based research to enhance quality first teaching skills for all children in a classroom. Its aim is to broaden the knowledge base of health and education practitioners with regards to the importance of promoting inclusion and participation in activities that affect pupil progress, including handwriting, self-care tasks, such as managing lunchtime and participation in physical activities and play.

Throughout the book 'Try this' sections have been included that aim to encourage readers to reflect on their own experience and to apply ideas and knowledge in their own setting/context – for trainees, reflective accounts could contribute to or form the basis of a personal portfolio of learning. Working with parents and carers is of course vital for all professionals and Chapter 5 provides ideas and strategies to support this work. However, we also wanted to show that parents and carers can be fully involved in all aspects of their child's development. To highlight this, blue text is used throughout the book whenever parents and carers are mentioned. They are of course the 'golden thread' crucial for a child's holistic physical and cognitive development in the Early Years.

By implementing the guidance in this book readers will see how this approach to early movement and coordination development can:

- help improve progress and academic achievement for all children;
- develop practitioner confidence in supporting the motor and coordination difficulties of children within an educational setting;

- embed a holistic approach to early learning and teaching, recognising the links between physical, social and communication, and cognitive development within the generic curriculum;
- support an integrated approach to Continuing Professional Development across professional boundaries; and
- provide parents with an understanding of the importance of motor and coordination development on children's academic progress.

Finally, it is hoped that the suggestions provided in this book will limit the need for small group targeted interventions or support and help to further enhance inclusive practice.

Introduction

It is estimated that between 2 and 6% of school-aged children experience difficulties with movement and coordination that affect their education and life chances. While some children have significant difficulties which will require specialist help, it is felt that many children with mild/moderate difficulties can be supported effectively through universal provision (Cleaton *et al.* 2020, Harrowell *et al.* 2018) in nurseries and schools by educators who know how to adapt the environment or implement new strategies and lessons.

This statistic is supported by a growing body of research which has found evidence between early motor problems and physical, social and cognitive difficulties (e.g. reading and speech and language) as children develop (Brown 2010; Rhemtulla and Tucker-Drob 2011). Also, there is a higher incidence of children from impoverished backgrounds who have movement and coordination difficulties due to fewer movement and play opportunities at home (World Health Organization 2019). Nurseries and early years settings are therefore crucially important environments, enabling all children to have access to activities which can help promote the development of movement and coordination skills and thus prevent children from starting school at a disadvantage.

This book therefore provides practitioners with the information and knowledge needed to tackle early motor developmental issues as part of universal Early Years' and Key Stage 1 provision.

This book is divided into five chapters each one looking at different aspects of early development learning. Each chapter can be read and accessed separately although links are made between the chapters when appropriate. A summary will be provided at the end of the chapters and a reference list can be found at the end of the book.

Chapter 1: Physical skills, movement and learning

In this chapter the key feature of motor learning will be explained, and ways to identify the children who would benefit from structured movement opportunities in order to facilitate their active participation in physical games and play will be explored.

This will help you understand:

- how movement can influence children's learning, achievement and self-esteem;
- how to observe children's movement and identify when a child may need more help;
- how to record and evaluate children's movement progress; and
- what resources are needed to run a movement and activity programme.

Physical activity in nursery settings/school is considered alongside an understanding of how a child learns to move. The importance of the Early Years' environment on children's movement development and the benefits and limitations of movement programmes will be discussed. Crucially, links between movement and learning will be highlighted and how you can observe children's movement will be explored. A movement observation checklist is provided, as well as some general principles which can be applied when thinking about the role of activity/programmes. The chapter ends with a discussion about the importance of recording each child's progress and the importance of sharing this information with parents and any other professionals involved in the child's development.

Chapter 2: Personal independence skills for learning and participation

This chapter will provide you with information, activities and practice suggestions about:

- which skills children need to be able to participate at lunchtimes in educational environments;
- developing social skills for lunchtimes in preschool settings and school;
- information about a range of resources and how to use them;
- when children are ready to dress themselves and basic dressing skills;
- how to help children get changed for PE; and
- the skills needed for young children to be able to use the toilet independently.

It will help you identify the skills children need to positively participate in mealtimes and will provide suggestions which will help encourage the development of cutlery use (internationally and culturally relevant) and social skills. Importantly, it will also tell you how these skills are helpful to aid handwriting development. Observation checklists, reflection opportunities and information about, for example, oral motor skills will be provided always highlighting the links between physical and educational development. There will be activities and advice about how to help children develop the skills to dress and undress themselves. There will also be help with understanding how we can enable children gain the skills necessary to use the toilet independently.

Chapter 3: Are they sitting comfortably?

This third chapter focuses on seating in the classroom, and the important role it plays within an educational environment and therefore a child's learning. It will explain how children develop postural control, the influence of good seating on attention and learning, and include classroom strategies and ideas to try. By the end of this chapter you will have the answers to the following questions:

- What do we mean by 'posture'?
- Why is appropriate seating important for a child's learning?
- Are there guidelines for good sitting in class?
- What is the impact of sitting on attention and learning? and
- How does classroom design influence learning?

Also, the reasons why some children have difficulties sitting are discussed and ideas how to resolve them are suggested. This information will be shared through activities, illustrations and case study examples.

Chapter 4: Confident handwriting

'Confident handwriting' will assist you in thinking about the skills children need before they can achieve confident and well-structured handwriting. The role of large, as well as fine motor skills, posture and attention skills, in the development of handwriting will all be explained here. The importance of recognising differences between children who are left- and right-handed is also discussed and helpful strategies are suggested.

As in previous chapters, activities and illustrations, as well as evidence-informed research, will be used to emphasise how 'handwriting' cannot and should not be seen as a separate skill from other movement and coordination skills.

Chapter 5: Working together with parents and carers

It is intended that you should use information in this chapter of the book as and when you require it for discussions with parents and carers (and other staff members). Throughout the book you will notice that there are sentences which are written in blue print. All of these are about parent partnership working and provide a 'golden thread' of evidence about the importance of working together with parents for all aspects of a child's educational experience. Unlike the previous chapters it will focus on providing suggestions and ideas and on how to signpost parents to support in order to encourage and involve them in their children's development and progress at nursery or school. These will help you demonstrate how important physical activity is for their children's academic futures, as well as their physical development.

Chapter 1: Physical skills, movement and learning

This chapter is about the development of physical skills in young children, the importance of activity in early childhood and the links between movement and children's learning. The aim of this chapter is to consider the influence of physical movement and activity on children's learning, self-esteem, health and wellbeing.

In this chapter there are suggestions about:

1. Ideas for creating movement opportunities for all children, promoting the link between physical activity and children's learning, self-esteem, health and wellbeing.
2. Observing children's movement skills.
3. Ways to support children that find physical skills, such as kicking or catching a ball, difficult or challenging.

Physical activity in Early Years education

Concerns about rising levels of obesity amongst children and low levels of physical activity have prompted initiatives such as 'the daily mile' – where children leave their classroom for 15 minutes a day to jog or run together. There are many other targeted sports and playground schemes designed for inclusion in Early Years and school settings that aim to increase the amount of physical activity young children engage in.

The benefits to children's long-term health and wellbeing of regular participation in activities that promote physical activity are now widely accepted e.g. maintaining a healthy weight and improved cardiovascular health (World Health Organization 2019). Other benefits such as the impact of physical activity on the development of coordination and control and the influence of movement on learning, confidence and mental health are currently less well understood (Fedewa and Ahn 2011; Howells and Sääkslahti 2019).

Some children will find it difficult to participate in games and lessons that involve physical skills when they begin their Early Years education. There may have been few opportunities in their early life to play outdoors or visit a playground and many will have

6 Physical skills, movement and learning

experienced predominantly sedentary leisure activities such as watching television at home. Others may have a specific difficulty, disability or delay in their development making physical activity more challenging.

Introducing daily, fun opportunities to practise physical movement skills can assist all children, including those with difficulties, to develop the skills needed to be included in Early Years education. For example, the National Health Service, *Change4Life* website (www.nhs.uk/change4life/about-change4life) promotes ten-minute physical activities designed to appeal to all children that can be easily incorporated into daily routines (National Health Service 2020). Such approaches may also have longer term benefits for children's learning (Mavilidi *et al.* 2016; Mullender-Wijnsma *et al.* 2015).

Try this

Take the opportunity to observe children during playtime. Are there children who avoid taking part in games that involve catching and throwing or kicking a ball or jumping and skipping? Then ask yourself these questions:

1. Do these children lack confidence in their physical skills? Do they avoid these activities because they cannot move or perform skills such as jumping as well as other children of their age? Or are there other reasons that might explain their reluctance to participate?
2. Are they overlooked by other children because they cannot kick or catch a ball?
3. What impact do you think not being involved in playground games and activities might have on their confidence, self-esteem and social skills?

To help you think about this from a child's point of view, reflect for a moment on your own skills.

1. Were you someone who mastered physical skills easily, or was it more difficult for you to participate in games and sports at school?
2. How did this influence your experiences at school?
3. Have these early experiences affected the lifestyle and leisure choices you have made as an adult?

There are several guidelines available to support greater levels of physical activity amongst young children. These include:

- *The UK's Chief Medical Officer* recommends 180 minutes of movement each day for children from birth to five years old, including activities such as object play, tummy time, dancing and messy play (United Kingdom, Chief Medical Officer 2019).
- *The WHO Guidelines* on physical activity, sedentary behaviour and sleep for children under the age of five recommends that children should:
  - Participate in a variety of physical activities for at least 180 minutes a day, with 60 minutes of moderate to vigorous activity.
  - Not have more than one hour of screen time, preferably less.
  - Have 10–13 hours of good quality sleep and wake times.

- *The World Health Organization* (2019) recommends 60 minutes a day of moderate to vigorous intensity physical activity daily for children aged five to 17 years of age.

How do children develop their movement skills?

The process of learning new movement and motor skills is most easily observed in young children when they are learning to crawl and walk. Children will practise the movement sequences required thousands and thousands of times as their bodies, muscles and balance mature. Learning to walk and other 'core' physical skills such as sitting and balance develop in an orderly sequence for a typically developing child, hence the idea of measuring a child's progress in terms of 'milestones' or stages (Sharma and Cockerill 2014). It is important to remember however that the pace and sequence of development varies from one child to another. For example, in the case of walking, some early walkers will take their first steps at nine months while others take longer to acquire this skill, with most learning to walk at around 12 months. The child's environment and opportunities for play are important factors influencing how young children develop.

There are thought to be *three stages* to learning a new motor skill. Take the example of riding a bike.

First stage: the child needs to have the opportunity and motivation to want to learn and an appreciation or understanding of what is required. For example, understanding how to propel the bike forwards by pressing on the pedals and how to stop the bike by applying the brakes.

Second stage: as the child practises these skills, they will use trial and error and their problem-solving skills to cope with new challenges, for example navigating differing terrain, turning corners etc.

Third stage: with practice and over time, the skill of riding a bike becomes effortless and automatic. There is no longer a need to 'think' about what is happening and the child can then focus attention on other things as they continue to pedal and steer.

Physical skills like riding a bike, learnt within the child's everyday context leads to the development of new abilities and behaviour. For example, being able to ride a bike means the child has the possibility of riding a bike to school which in turn builds independence and responsibility. Developing any movement skill involves *motivation* and *active concentration* on the part of the child and the *opportunity to practise* within a safe and supportive environment. We can continue to learn new physical skills throughout our lives. As we often find learning easier in situations where we learn alongside others, the social dimension of motor learning is an important aspect to consider when developing opportunities for young children to build their skills (Wolpert *et al.* 2001).

Try this

When did you last master a new skill?
Have you learnt to salsa dance or drive recently?
Have you taken up a new hobby such as learning to play a musical instrument?

8 Physical skills, movement and learning

Reflect on the following questions and think about how you can encourage the children you work with as they go through the stages of learning new skills.

What did it feel like to learn a new skill? Were you nervous or anxious? How many times did you have to practise this skill before it became automatic? When the task was difficult were you tempted to give up? What kept you motivated?

Your own experiences will give you an insight into what it is like for children who find it difficult to learn a new skill – whether learning to catch or kick a ball or learning how to write. Reflecting on your own experience will help you develop creative ways of assisting the children you work with in their learning.

Encourage parents to introduce physical activities at home at weekends and during the school holidays and breaks. Something as simple as going out for a walk or going to the park. There are ideas to promote cycling and swimming in Chapter 5.

How does the environment affect children's physical development?

Many children start Early Years education and school with fewer movement skills today (2020), compared to a decade ago. Agility, coordination and balance are fundamental skills required for young children to be able to learn effectively at school. The increasing number of children with difficulties with movement has been attributed to:

- Lack of opportunities to play – access to open outdoor spaces and playgrounds.
- Changes in parenting styles and habits – avoidance of risks, little encouragement to play and explore outdoors.
- Changes in society and culture – sedentary lifestyles, passive leisure activities.
- Social disadvantage – children from disadvantaged backgrounds are more likely to have delayed skills (Buttle UK 2019).

How can we promote the development of core movement skills in young children and assist those children who struggle?

It is important that all those working with young children understand:

- how they learn to move;
- how to help children who struggle; and
- how to maintain the interest and motivation of children.

These are important factors that are known to affect a child's participation and inclusion (Sharma and Cockerill 2014).

Offering children regular and consistent opportunities to practise movement skills – including opportunities to balance and develop their agility and coordination can help all children to participate in playground games, physical activities (PE) and sports in Early Years.

Consider using a 'small steps' approach by breaking down more complex physical skills such as kicking a ball into simpler tasks so that all children can be included. Think about incorporating counting and rhythm into activities to stimulate children's cognitive abilities (Tomporowski *et al.* 2015).

A 'small steps' approach

Using a 'small steps' approach means that complex skills such as kicking a ball are first broken into component elements – e.g. shifting weight from one leg to another and balancing on one leg before kicking the ball. Building physical movement skills in this way enables a young child to gradually develop their confidence in the following areas:

- Large movements e.g. skipping, running.
- Balance skills.
- Ball skills, catching, throwing.
- Planning and coordination e.g. climbing frame, obstacle course.
- Fine motor skills e.g. activities that involve both hands working together, such as threading, using scissors.
- Body awareness e.g. the position of the body in relation to what is around you.

Some ideas using a 'small steps' approach

Balancing

Most of us have a dominant or preference for using our right or left hand. We will also have a preferred leg when we balance and therefore balancing on one leg will be easier on one leg compared with the other (Try this for yourself. Which is your dominant leg?). If you kick a ball, your dominant leg will be the leg that you choose without thinking to balance on. Not everyone finds balancing easy. How long can you balance on one leg?

On starting Early Years education children will be developing their balance skills and will be able to balance briefly on either foot. Remember that all children develop differently between the ages of three and four years, hence some children will be more skilled in this respect than others.

Standing on one leg

Step one – shift weight from one leg to another.
Step two – focus on a point straight ahead and level with your eyes.
Step three – slowly lift one foot off the floor.
Step four – put hands out to steady yourself.
Step five – maintain position for as long as you can.

Physical skills, movement and learning

To make the task easier

Hold hands with the child and balance on one foot together.
Ask the child to hold onto a chair or the wall.
Lift the foot only slightly off the floor.
Practise other balance activities such as walking with big strides, stepping over different types of PE equipment boxes, hula hoops etc.

To make the task harder

Balance for longer.
Balance on either leg.
Balance with eyes closed.
Balance on a wobbly or soft surface.
Lift hands over your head.
Reach out of the 'base of support'.

What is the 'base of support'?

We feel stable and balanced when our body is in contact with the ground and aligned with the line of gravity. Imagine a line running from the centre of your head through the body to the ground, that is known as the 'line of gravity'. When we move out of our base of support to perhaps reach for something, we need to make compensatory movements to prevent ourselves from falling. This ability to move in and out of the base of support develops through play and active movement in young children.

Catching a ball

There are some prerequisite motor skills that a child needs to have before they can catch a ball. Children will be developing their throwing and catching skills around three or four years of age. Some questions to ask when you are observing children's ball skills are:

- Can the child follow the trajectory of a ball or beanbag with their eyes?
- Can they concentrate long enough to catch the ball or are they distracted by other things happening in the room?
- Can they bring their hands together in a smooth, steady way?
- Can they stabilise their lower body?
- Can they raise their arms and hands without losing their balance?
- Can they shift their balance and move comfortably in and out of their base of support?

Typical steps involved in catching a ball

1. Step one – child stands with feet hip distance apart.
2. Step two – hold both hands out ready to catch.
3. Step three – watches the trajectory of the ball or beanbag.
4. Step four – adjusts position of the body in line with direction of the ball.
5. Step five – brings hands together to catch the ball.

To make the task easier

- Stand behind the child, place your hands over their arms, bring their arms together as the ball comes towards them.
- Choose a large ball that is slightly deflated, or a beanbag.
- Throw at very close range.
- Throw directly towards the child.
- Catch the ball with the whole of the body.

To make the task harder

- Choose a smaller ball.
- Throw at greater range.
- Throw ball to left or right upwards or lower (the child moves out of their base of support).
- Catch with the palm of the hands and fingers only.
- Catch with only one hand.

Jumping

Children develop the ability to jump with two feet together.

Step one – stand with feet together.
Step two – bend knees.
Step three – push down and lift body upwards simultaneously.
Step four – land on the ground (feet not together).
Step five – land with feet together.

To make the task easier

Hold hands with the child and jump together.
Use music to help with rhythm.
Use a small step/book to jump from.

To make the task harder

Jump over obstacles.
Bunny jumps.

12 Physical skills, movement and learning

What are the benefits?

- Regular timetabled opportunities can promote development of core skills e.g. balance, affecting the child's ability to sit and maintain attention during class. (Refer to Chapter 3 'Are they sitting comfortably?').
- Improve coordination of large and precision motor skills.
- Have a positive impact on a child's self-esteem and confidence.
- Establish enjoyment of movement and activity – that may promote the child's long-term health and wellbeing.

Try this

To help you understand how we learn and adapt our physical skills:

1. Get used to the sensitivity mouse settings on your computer.
2. Change the sensitivity setting.
3. Practise using this new setting for ten minutes.
4. Now turn the sensitivity back on again.

You will find that when you change the settings it feels 'wrong' and you keep overshooting or undershooting the icon that you are looking for. As you practise you will get better at dealing with the new settings until it feels normal again. Then when you change back you will find that it feels wrong again.

What is going on? When you start to use the mouse your brain sends signals to individual muscles guiding the amount and direction of movement required. If this has the desired result, then the brain will use the same set of signals next time.

If you change the sensitivity of the mouse, your brain will need to alter these signals to make the movement work again. However, the learning only works for the movements that you have practised. If you try using the other hand or a different movement, you will have to relearn this skill.

This exercise provides an insight into why children with motor delay or difficulties benefit from regular opportunities to practise their movement skills. Children should be actively engaged in the process of learning motor skills. Inviting children to assess their own performance and movement responses will help them to identify solutions that can help them improve these skills. Asking open questions such as 'How did that go?' 'What might make it easier?' can help children think about their own response to movement challenges (Dawson *et al.* 2017). Encourage parents to practise catching and throwing at home – if space is limited practising with a soft ball or balloon can help children develop the coordination skills needed.

Note: *You should seek the advice of a state registered occupational therapist and/or physiotherapist for children with complex movement difficulties and those children with a diagnosed physical disability such as cerebral palsy.*

Links between movement and learning

Movement can help the child gain greater awareness of their environment. Children learn about their bodies by interacting with and moving through their environment. This ability to know where we are in relation to the things around us is called 'body awareness'. As children learn to move and interact with their environment, they begin to understand how much force is needed to move an object and how and where to position themselves to achieve what they want or need to do. You will notice that children with less developed body awareness will have difficulties throwing or catching a ball, for example, throwing with too much or with insufficient force. They may also be more likely to bump into tables and chairs in the classroom and stand or sit too close to or too far away from other children.

It is large (or gross) physical movements that precede the development of fine or precision skills such as pencil control in typical motor development (Sugden and Wade 2013). Large motor patterns in the body, arms and shoulders help to stabilise the body to allow the fine, precision and small motor movements of the hands and fingers. Hence a child needs good stability in their shoulders and the ability to maintain a comfortable seated posture as a precursor to learning to write (Schneck and Amundson 2010) (see Chapter 4 for more about handwriting skills). Also, they may have difficulty sitting still in one position for even quite short periods of time or be unable to listen and sit cross-legged at the same time. It is in these ways therefore that less developed motor skills can impact on a child's ability to learn as effectively as possible.

The development of movement and physical skills are closely linked to the child's maturing sensory abilities. Taking a holistic view of a child's development can help understanding of the interrelatedness of movement to learning and sensory awareness. We use the term sensory in its broadest sense here to include not only vision and hearing but also a sense of balance (vestibular), touch (tactile) and sense of self in space (body awareness/proprioception). These sensory 'abilities' develop through play and exploration of the child's environment. An example of the integration of the sensory and motor systems is how a child learns to play on a swing. The child must use all the senses outlined above to move the swing successfully.

Some children find some movement sensations unpleasant and may avoid certain physical activities. Examples are swinging or climbing up or going down a slide. With patient support children may overcome aversions to movement or other sensations. We all have differing responses to sensation and this is natural, contributing to our personal preferences and identity. A problem only occurs where a response (such as when a child is afraid of lifting their feet off the ground) affects a child's ability to engage in the activities they need to take part in Early Years education (Connell and McCarthy 2013).

Observing children moving

An understanding of typical physical development in young children can help you judge whether a child lacks maturity or has more significant difficulties that may require professional help from a member of the multidisciplinary team (Sharma and Cockerill

2014; Sugden and Wade 2013). Understanding the stages and processes of motor development will help you identify when to intervene and provide more help for a child who may be struggling (Howard 2017). Intervention of the right type is very important in terms of maintaining children's confidence and self-esteem.

Try this

If you are concerned about a child, observe them in a variety of nursery- or school-based activities identified in the **Movement observation checklist** (Table 1.1). Observe the child in different environments such as the classroom, playground or dining hall. Make detailed notes about what you are observing and how the child's behaviour is affected. Should you need to refer to a member of the multidisciplinary team this type of information can be very helpful in determining the best way to help the child.

There are many different small steps movement programmes designed for use in Early Years and school settings that aim to promote the development of core or fundamental movement skills in young children. Some programmes are designed to be used with individual children and others are intended for whole group, class or whole school use. Some programmes require those responsible for leading the programme to attend a training session.

When considering whether to make use of a movement programme check that you understand the reasoning underpinning its use and that it is based on contemporary and current understanding about how children develop. This knowledge will influence how the programme is implemented and help you evaluate its effectiveness (Eddy *et al.* 2019; Brian and Taunton 2018).

Table 1.1 Movement observation checklist

Name: DOB: School:

Before running the programme answer the following questions for the children

Can the child carry out the following skills?	Needs further practice	Satisfactory	Good	Where observed
Running				
Jumping				
Ball skills				
Scissor skills				
Concentrating				
Changing for PE				
Using cutlery				
Balancing				
General organisation				

Is there a time of day that these difficulties are most apparent? If yes, when?	YES/NO
Does the child have a physical disability or medical condition?	YES/NO

NB. If 'yes' refer to a Therapy service for advice before commencing motor programme.

(*Continued*)

Physical skills, movement and learning

AFTER running the programme ask yourself the following questions:
Which movement programme has been used?
How many sessions a week did the child take part in?
How long did each session last (approximately)?
In which areas has the child progressed well and when did they struggle?

Can the child carry out the following skills?	Needs further practice	Satisfactory	Good	Where observed
Running				
Jumping				
Ball skills				
Scissor skills				
Concentrating				
Changing for PE				
Using cutlery				
Balancing				
General organisation				
Other:				

Also, describe parent involvement in supporting programme:
Plan for development:

Try this

Go through the general principles below and check that you are considering these aspects when designing or planning physical activities.

- Always start at a level where children can experience success. This may differ between children in the class, so ensure that every child can be successful at some point. 'The just right challenge' means the point where a child can succeed but is also challenged so they can progress further.
- Modify activities so that they are achievable. For example, when catching a ball choose a larger ball or make the distance smaller to make the task easier for some children.
- Use a small steps approach. Allow a child to master a skill before introducing a more difficult challenge. For example, balancing on one leg before kicking a ball.
- Give children lots or praise, encouragement and constructive feedback.
- Involve children in choosing activities that are important and help them to evaluate their own progress. For example, say 'How did that go?' 'Can you think about how to make this better?'
- Encourage children to suggest ways as to how they can improve their own performance. Where children struggle, give constructive verbal and visual feedback. 'Try bending like this' then demonstrate – 'like this.'
- You may need to place the child's limbs or body in a position for them to 'feel' what the movement is like.
- Make activities fun and exciting. For example, 'let's jump like a frog! How high can you jump?'

- Allow regular opportunities to practise. Little and often is the rule. Three or four times a week for 10–15 minutes is better than once a week for half an hour.
- Involve families and parents so that the child can be encouraged to practise skills at home and during holidays.

Recording children's progress

Interventions aimed at improving movement abilities in young children need to be monitored to ensure that children are making progress. If they are not making progress, then a different approach needs to be taken and this may be the time to ask for professional help from the multidisciplinary team.

Be clear about what you are expecting a child to achieve and within what time frame. Involve children directly in setting their own goals and encourage them to assess their progress. Remember you might also want to include parents in this decision making.

Outcomes should be linked to participation in everyday school activities. For example, learning to kick a ball so that the child can play football with friends at playtime. Help the child to make the link between the skills they are working on and what they want to achieve. For example, doing up buttons will enable them to get changed for physical education (PE) independently. This may also be an important outcome for parents, who would really appreciate their child being able to do up their own clothes in a busy household (go to Chapter 2 for more information about developing independence).

Summary

This chapter has considered the importance of movement to children's learning and ways to provide regular opportunities for all children to practise their movement skills.

Reflect on what you have learnt and consider how you could put into practice ideas presented in this chapter. Can you answer the questions below?

Do you agree that many children start Early Years education with fewer movement and physical skills than a decade ago?
What are some of the reasons given for this?
How would you describe the 'base of support'?
Why is it important for children to be able to move in and out of their base of support?
What underpins the development of fine or precision skills involving the hands?

Chapter 2: Personal independence skills for learning and participation

This chapter of the book explores the personal independence skills that young children are required to master during their Early Years education. Being able to use the toilet, undress and dress themselves, and eat a healthy meal are essential to children's participation, learning, health and wellbeing. Many children acquire these skills at home with the support of their families, but not all children do. This chapter provides practical suggestions and ideas for Early Years practitioners who want to support all the children in their group or class, including those who have difficulty gaining personal independence skills.

Firstly, it is important to remember that children want to be independent and take pride in being able to 'do things for themselves' whether putting on their own coat and shoes or cutting up their food at mealtimes. It is equally important to remember that it is good to let them practise such tasks, because whilst they are learning these skills they are also developing the physical coordination they need to help them learn in the classroom. For example, practice and motivation will also help children use tools such as scissors and pencils, and to develop spatial, planning and sequencing skills, all of which contribute to their educational progress.

The chapter is divided into three parts:

1. 'Second helpings' focuses on mealtimes and making healthy food choices.
2. 'Dress to impress' considers how children learn to dress and provides advice about changing clothes before taking part in physical education sessions.
3. 'Using the loo' discusses independence in personal hygiene and how to create a comfortable environment for children when they use the toilet.

Try this: Reflect on when you last attended a meeting or an event in an unfamiliar setting. Before getting to the business of the day you probably thought first about where the toilets were, where to leave your coat and what you would be having for lunch! We take for granted the complex motor and coordination skill required when engaging in these everyday tasks often until an injury or disability affects us. Having to relearn a skill helps us remember how much effort is required.

Second helpings

Lunchtime is an important, but often neglected part of the school day, providing space for children to visit the toilet, eat a healthy meal with their peers and play. Over the past 20 years as the pressure on school timetables has increased, school break times have been shortened, and in some cases lunchtimes are limited to 35 minutes (Baines and Blatchford 2019).

Nutritionally, lunchtime affords children who have started their day early and possibly without breakfast, an opportunity to refuel. Nutrition in early childhood and throughout the child's school years influences cognitive development, behaviour and productivity. Conversely, the effects of poor nutrition are long lasting with longitudinal studies demonstrating negative effects on school achievement extending into adolescence (Prado and Dewey 2014). Observations from a review of poverty in the UK found that children who are hungry are less able to cope with the challenges of each school day. They are more likely to struggle emotionally – becoming withdrawn, depressed, angry and detached from life. School meals offer an important lifeline for many disadvantaged children and families (Joseph Rowntree Foundation 2018; Wickramasinghe *et al.* 2017).

As with dressing and learning to use the toilet, we cannot assume that young children by the time they start Early Years education, will have acquired the skills to be able to sit at a table, manipulate eating utensils, understand the routines associated with eating, such as washing hands and have the social skills to share a meal with their peers. Early Years education offers the chance for all children to develop skills that are important for social acceptance and participation in life (Bruns and Thompson 2014; Graham *et al.* 2015).

This chapter will:

- Focus on the developmental stages linked to the skills children need to be able to participate in school mealtimes.
- Explore why some children struggle with the skills associated with eating a meal.

Why is lunchtime important?

Children arrive at school with a variety of eating experiences influenced by their social, cultural and ethnic background. Some children will regularly sit at a table with their family to eat at home, whilst others will have more experience of eating 'on the go' or with a tray on their lap in front of the television. Eating can be a positive experience where we share food with friends and family, but changes in family routines over the last decade suggest that fewer families regularly eat a family meal together and children may never experience this type of family meal at home (Jones 2018).

Children may eat alone and may not recognise eating as a social activity or have support to develop their eating and chewing skills such as learning how to eat and chew with their mouth closed. Many will not have been taught how to manipulate the utensils associated with preparing and eating food including handling knives, forks, spoons, plates and cups. Greater independence at mealtimes offers children opportunities to interact with their peers leading to the formation of friendships, self-esteem and confidence. Understanding how to make healthy choices at mealtimes is also important as young children develop preferences for different food types, tastes and textures.

It is important to remember that family mealtimes can be influenced by:

- Work patterns and home routines which may make it difficult for families to sit down together at mealtimes.
- Lack of physical space for a dining table.
- Changes in meal structure and ideas about what constitutes a 'healthy' meal.
- Greater use of convenience food.

Personal independence skills for learning and participation

- Snacking and eating 'on the go'.
- Cultural and ethnic influences affecting diet and routine.
- Food poverty (The Children's Society 2019).

Early Years settings need to consider how they can support parents and carers in helping their children develop the eating and social skills necessary to enable them to participate in a range of different mealtime experiences that children are likely to encounter at home, school and in the wider community. Ofsted (2019) also feel it is important that Early Years settings carefully consider their approach to supporting children's personal development, behaviour and welfare, including how to promote children's confidence, independence and understanding about how to keep themselves physically and mentally healthy.

Try this

Observe children eating their cooked or packed lunches. Identify whether some children are having difficulty – with sitting, cutting their food, chewing and swallowing their food or appear to be 'messy' or 'picky' eaters.

- Do they dribble excessively? Cough or choke on their food? Stuff food into their mouth? Get food on their face or drop food on their clothing or the floor?
- Do some children leave a lot of food, take a long time to eat?
- Are some children left at the table long after other children have left the table to play?
- Are some children in frequent trouble with lunchtime staff?

Bearing in mind what is known about the importance of nutrition to concentration and attention what impact do you think that these difficulties or issues are likely to have on a child's nutrition, their ability to digest a meal, their learning, self-esteem and social skills?

Try this: reflect on your own skills

Imagine you are on holiday in a foreign country. You are invited for dinner in someone's home. None of the eating implements are familiar to you? You don't know what the routines are or how you are expected to behave. You are very likely to feel anxious and make some mistakes. How would you feel being corrected and what help would you like your hosts to give to you to make the meal a pleasurable experience?

Now reflect on how you respond to children in your nursery or school who may have similar problems. How do you respond to their anxieties or mistakes?

A closer look at your Early Years dining area

Limited time can make school lunchtime rushed and stressful. The dining area can be very noisy and some children with sensitivities to noise and smell can feel overwhelmed. Expectations from lunchtime staff and teachers about appropriate behaviour may not be clear or may be unrealistic. All these factors influence a child's experience of lunchtime, of eating food and by association how comfortable they are.

Personal independence skills for learning and participation — 20

Try this

Think back to your own experience of 'school dinners' as a child.

- What memories do you have? Are they positive or negative? Did your experiences of lunchtime shape your own likes or dislikes of certain foods?
- Can you recall the dining hall at your school? Can you recall the sounds and smells? How would you describe these?
- Carry out an observation of lunchtimes as they are currently organised at your school. Use the accompanying checklist as a starting point.
- Once you have completed your observation consider with your colleagues ways that together you could improve the lunchtime experience for everyone. Don't forget to talk to the children themselves as they will most probably have great ideas (Children's Food Trust 2013; Dimbleby and Vincent 2014).

To make these changes think about:

- What resources do you need?
- Who needs to be involved?
- What needs to be changed?

Improvements could involve:

- Moving the furniture to make larger spaces.
- Make sure chairs and tables are the appropriate height for the children.
- Staggering lunchtime to allow more space for children.
- Teachers sharing their lunch with the children.
- Older children sharing or supporting younger children.
- Developing lunchtime guidelines with the children about behaviour and expectations.
- Ensuring that utensils, plates and cups fully support all age groups and both left and right handed children.

Look at the lunchtime checklist. This will help you to think of the questions you need to ask and aid your observations.

What skills does a child need at lunchtime?

At the age children start Early Years education they would be expected to be able to maintain a stable head position to chew and swallow and be able to enjoy a wide range of foods of different tastes and textures. Children will be imitating the eating behaviour of peers and adults and forming their own food preferences, based on taste and texture of foods they like or dislike. Most children will have the ability to be able to sit at a table and have the coordination skills to manipulate a range of eating utensils. For example, be able to use a fork and spoon and pour a drink into a beaker with some spilling. Some will be starting to use a knife and fork with support.

Provision of suitable seating is important when children are eating. Children should have their feet placed on the floor or a firm surface. The dining table needs to be at a functional height (comfortable elbow height). This is important because the child's body needs to be stable for children to be able to use eating utensils and the head needs to be balanced for children to chew and swallow effectively.

Table 2.1 Lunchtime observation checklist

Observations	Comments	Ideas
Seating What are the seating arrangements? Draw a diagram to represent layout Are children seated with feet on floor and tables correct height? How much space is available for each child?		
Environment How noisy is the dining hall? Does this appear to affect any of the children?		
Social Are the children able to speak with each other? How much communication happens? What are children talking about?		
Behavioural Is behaviour an issue at lunchtime?		
Time How long is lunchtime? Is it rushed?		
Cutlery Is the cutlery the right size and shape for the children to use comfortably? How many children are using cutlery well? How many are having difficulty? How do staff assist children with their cutlery skills?		

22 Personal independence skills for learning and participation

It is often the case that school dining furniture may provide insufficient postural support for young children. For example, folding tables with stools attached provide very limited support, stools that rotate making them unstable and if they are a fixed height, children of differing heights cannot be accommodated easily. Where possible choose furniture that enables children to sit comfortably on a stable surface with their feet firmly on the floor.

Try this

Imagine you are in a bar or restaurant sitting on a high bar stool with your legs dangling. If you are trying to eat a meal with a knife and fork your legs will probably start to search for support – you may try to stabilise yourself by hooking your legs around the stool legs. How do you 'feel' in this position? Being unstable can have an effect on how you eat and your enjoyment of a meal. We all know how difficult it is at a party to stand and eat with a wobbly plate and glass in our hands! The first thing you would do is to search for somewhere comfortable to sit.

During your observation of lunchtime routines also think about whether:

- Some children are finding it difficult to sit still and upright.
- You can improve the seating options for children, bearing in mind the different heights and sizes of children by choosing different table and chair combinations.

Children need to be able to coordinate both hands when using eating utensils such as a knife and fork or spoon and fork. Each hand has a specific role to play when they work together. A good way to explain this to children is to say there is a 'doer' hand and a 'helper' hand. The knife for example is the 'doer' hand and the fork the 'helper' hand that holds the food still or steady. Both left and right-handed children can understand this.

For children who haven't used a knife and fork before you should demonstrate how to hold cutlery by placing the index fingers on the top edge of the knife and fork handles, with the remaining fingers and thumb wrapped around the handle. For some children it may be helpful to place coloured stickers to mark the correct finger position place.

Using a knife and fork together is called a 'bilateral' hand task – involving both hands working together in

Personal independence skills for learning and participation

a coordinated way. Practicing other tasks that involve bilateral coordination, such as cutting and sticking and rolling and cutting out dough can help in the development of cutlery and other bilateral skills that are important for schoolwork.

Try this

Experiment yourself with the 'doer' and 'helper' hand. But swap the hands you normally use to hold the knife and fork – notice how difficult it is to relearn this skill. Remember how this felt and what helped when you are encouraging children to develop their hand skills.

- Did you have to concentrate very hard?
- Did you need to watch what you were doing?
- What helps you?
- Think back to your observations in the dining hall. How easy do you think it would be for children to practise these skills at lunchtime?
- How supportive are your rules and expectations for children trying to develop these skills?

Chewing and swallowing

Learning appropriate eating skills includes being able to chew food and swallow – chewing and swallowing in turn supports the development of a child's speech. It is important that children can use the muscles around the mouth, jaw and tongue through swallowing, chewing, blowing and sucking. Fun activities that involve these skills can help all children develop the coordination required to eat well without dribbling or gulping their food.

Try this

For Early Years and Key Stage 1 children the following ideas are fun ways to explore their mouths and speech sounds.

- Puffing out the cheeks; then sucking in the cheeks to make hollows.
- Blowing bubbles through a straw dipped in water.
- Try sucking up a piece of paper with a straw and make a game of this.

You can make up stories to help the tongue move in different ways and explore with the children the different sounds that make up speech.

A Tongue story

- Can Tongue see along the road? (Stick Tongue out to the left or right).
- Now can Tongue see along the road the other way (move Tongue in the other direction).
- Is the sky blue today? (Move Tongue up to the nose).
- Are there any puddles on the pavement? (Move Tongue down towards the chin).

Try this

Think about the last time you had a picnic and used paper plates and disposable cutlery. Does the food move around on the plate and the plate move on the table? How frustrating is this? Are you tempted to use your hands and fingers? Now try a ceramic plate and comfortable well-designed cutlery that fits your hands. Notice the difference. There is some evidence to suggest that diners who use heavier cutlery enjoy their food and say it tastes better than those use cheaper lightweight cutlery! We often give children poor quality adult sized eating utensils and plastic plates that make it more difficult to eat. Why?

How can you help if a child is struggling?

- The child who finds sitting at the dining table difficult – check the seating available, are their feet flat on the floor? Is the seat stable?
- Is the child struggling with coordination and utensil use? Is the cutlery the right size for small hands? Is the plate stable on the table? Have they been guided and shown how to use both hands together and how to hold utensils correctly?
- Children who have a diagnosed physical disability, for example cerebral palsy may need adapted cutlery at mealtimes – always seek the advice of a state registered occupational therapist if you are uncertain of their needs.

Try this

Provide opportunities in the classroom for children to practise cutting different types of materials. Make sure activities take into consideration a child's age. Discuss the amount of effort and skill required to cut a banana or a thin piece of paper and the difference in the amount of effort required to cut a piece of material or card. Modelling with play dough can provide opportunities to develop fine motor, grip and hand control and hand-eye coordination.

Dress to impress

The skills of dressing and undressing, learning how to fasten and unfasten zips and buttons, and tying shoelaces require sensory, motor, planning and sequencing skills. Being independent in dressing and undressing is crucial to a child's inclusion and participation at school. For example, it underpins a child's ability to take part in daily school routines, such as hanging up their coat on arrival at school, the social acceptance of being able to wear a school uniform, adjusting clothing after using the toilet and getting changed for physical education classes.

Most children learn to dress at home and parents and carers play an important role providing instruction and encouraging their children to participate in dressing routines from an early age. Parents encourage their children to build the skills required to undress and dress through play and by demonstration and providing instruction. Like most physical skills children need to practise these skills many, many times before becoming independent. However, not all children experience support at home, and children from disadvantaged backgrounds and those children with developmental delay, communication needs or disability may require assistance and more structured support to help them adjust to the demands of dressing and undressing at school. This section will consider:

- The typical developmental stages in dressing skills.
- How to promote independence in dressing and undressing for all children.

When do children learn to dress themselves?

Children acquire the skills to undress and dress between the ages of two and six. Realistic expectations about what children can achieve at various stages in their development is important, as is appreciation that children will vary in their developmental progress (Sharma and Cockerill 2014). The environment, particularly the support the child receives at home, is an important influence. Opportunities to practise the skills of dressing at home and encouragement and praise for effort are important determinants of success.

From the age of 12 months onwards children begin to show an interest in dressing, for example, assisting by putting out an arm when pulling on a cardigan or a leg when pulling on trousers. Young babies, on discovering their feet, will remove their socks and will pull off and try to put on a soft hat. By the ages of two and a half to three years children are showing an interest in dressing themselves. For example, they might attempt to undo large buttons, pull on socks and put on their shoes. At this age they still require assistance with dressing and are likely to struggle with identifying front and back, right and left and haven't yet acquired the coordination needed to align buttons and fasten zips.

By the age of four many will be able to undress themselves such as pulling off T-shirts and pants, and they will be starting to dress themselves, although they will still require help with fastenings. Between the ages of five and six children are becoming more competent, their coordination and manipulative skills enabling them to fasten buttons and zips. They start to understand left and right and front and back and are less likely to get clothes the wrong way, or back to front.

More complex skills, such as tying shoelaces may not be mastered until the ages of six to seven or even later. Tying shoelaces is no longer a daily requirement for children as footwear includes styles without laces. However, being able to tie laces and tie a school tie is an important 'rite of passage' and as children mature having the option of wearing laced up shoes is important especially at secondary level. Imagine not being able to fasten football or hockey boots? Hence practicing these skills is still important.

Try this

Make a mental note of all the skills (motor, sensory, body awareness, planning sequencing etc) you needed this morning when getting yourself dressed. For example, being able to balance on one leg to put on pants, tights or trousers. Being able to coordinate both your hands together to fasten buttons. Being able to tolerate the 'feel' of your clothing next to your skin. Knowing the sequence of dressing i.e. that you need to put pants on before putting on your skirt or trousers.

Perceptual skills are very important when dressing – these skills help us to process and make sense of the visual information we receive. Perception is *interpreting* what we see when we use our vision. It enables us to find the right items of clothing, for example in a pile of clothes, locate an opening (arm hole, neck etc) and orientate clothes correctly on our bodies.

How do you think the skills needed to dress are relevant more generally to a child's education?

The skills needed to dress provide practice in balancing, individual control of our fingers, visual tracking, perceptual and sensory understanding, and precision and coordination. These skills support the development of sitting still, attention, participating in playground and other games, drawing, colouring and writing. By mastering such skills children are also accepted as part of the 'group' helping them to build social and emotional literacy skills and make friends.

Some basic dressing skills

Doing up buttons is a bilateral task that involve both hands working together. When children start learning to do buttons it is important to help them practise with large brightly coloured buttons and a hole that is big enough to push the button through with ease. After practising a great deal we don't need to look at a button to fasten it we can do this using touch alone but to start with children will need to rely on their vision. As with all independence skills making it a fun activity to practise will motivate children as will giving lots of feedback and praise. Don't forget to encourage parents to buy clothes for their children that have large buttons and button holes. In this way practice can take place at nursery or school and home.

Doing up a button

Step one

> Let's find the button.
> Then open the hole.

Push the button through the hole.
Grab the button.

Making the task easier

Practise doing up buttons when not wearing the garment.
Choose clothing with large buttons.
Start practising with buttons the child can see, e.g. at the bottom of a shirt.
Make sure the button hole is large enough.
Try 'hand over hand' technique.

Doing up a zip

Doing up a zip takes practise. Children will benefit from learning about how a zip works. First demonstrate and show the child how the zip goes up and down and practise pulling the zip up and down together.

Doing up a zip on the child

Step one – sit down.
Step two – put on the garment.
Step three – bring the two parts of the zip together.
Step four – hold the left part of the zip
Step five – push the right side down into the zip.
Step six – pull down with the right side while pulling up the zip tab.

Making the task easier

Sit down and practise together.
Use a hand over hand technique, your hand over the child's hand.
Choose a large zipper.
Put a tag, small toy or tape on the end of the zip to make it easier to hold
Practise doing up a zip when not wearing the garment.

Helping children getting changed for PE

When getting ready for PE children are practising all the motor and coordination skills identified above (balance, body awareness, perceptual, coordination). These skills are important to their overall development and by association their learning.

Observe the children in your class and their ability to undress and dress for PE. The following list will help you identify the children who are finding it hard, whilst also providing a good scaffold for all the children. Changing times can be very stressful for the adults so hopefully the following ideas will help everyone find these times more positive!

1. It is important to allow enough time for children to get themselves undressed and dressed. Don't try to rush as this will just end in everyone being unhappy and stressed.
2. It is easier to get dressed when sitting, especially when putting on pants and shorts. Encourage children to sit on a low chair or the floor when changing for PE.
3. Demonstrate how to get changed for PE. Go through each stage step by step. Have a visual aid or pictures to show the children what to do step by step and ask them to help you tell everyone what needs to be done next. This can be done for dressing and undressing.
4. Provide verbal prompts for each stage as children get changed.
5. Encourage the children to put their clothing into a bag/box or on a mat as they take off their clothes. This will make it easier for them to locate and find their clothes when it's time to get dressed.

It is always important to follow the same routine until everyone becomes confident. Develop a rhyme or song to accompany getting changed so that you are helping the children remember the steps in a happy rhythmic way.

Undressing song for PE

> I take off my jumper – and put it on my table
> I take off my shirt/blouse – and put it on the table with my jumper
> I take off my shoes and put them together under the table
> I take off my trousers/skirt – and put them with my jumper and shirt/blouse
> I then ….
> Put on my gym shorts
> Put on my gym shirt
> Put on my plimsolls
> And wave my hands in the air to show I am ready!

Dressing song for class

> I take off my gym shorts – and put them in my bag
> I take off my gym shirt – and put it in my bag
> I take off my plimsolls – and put them into my bag
> I then ….
> Put on my trousers/skirt
> Put on my blouse/shirt
> Put on my jumper
> Put on my shoes
> I'm ready!

Observe the children in your class dressing and undressing. Make a note of children who:

- Find it difficult to balance and fall over.
- Get the sequence of undressing and dressing muddled.

Personal independence skills for learning and participation

- Find it hard to 'tolerate' their clothing (complain that jumpers are itchy or labels scratchy).
- Struggle with coordination.
- Have difficulty because their clothes are ill fitting/ too small or inappropriate.

For these children the following will help give you some ideas.

Suggestions for helping children who are struggling with dressing and undressing

- Involve the child's parents in setting realistic targets and encourage practice at home as well as school.
- Ensure that children have clothing that is appropriate and fits them. It is easier to take off and put on clothing that is loose. Tight fitting pants and tops are harder to get on and off. Ask parents to help you with this.
- Set aside time for children to practise one skill at a time e.g. fastening buttons and provide regular opportunities for them to practise these skills throughout the day.
- Involve the child in choosing the skill they would like to master next.
- If working on buttons and zips, choose large buttons and zips to start with.
- Practise fastening the item of clothing when the child is not wearing it first before trying to fasten clothing on the body.
- Talk through the steps involved as you demonstrate using pictures, symbols or drawings to help you.
- Make practice time fun! There are commercial dressing dolls and toys that incorporate zips, buttons, laces and poppers to help children learn to dress. Or make your own props – for example take a large paper plate and make a slit in the centre large enough for the child to push through big buttons. Gather a range of large zips and clothes with large buttons. Make a dressing up box with all types of clothing in it.
- Put your hands over the child's hands to guide them as they carry out a skill such as learning to fasten a zip.
- Practise regularly and give the child lots of praise and encouragement.

Remember: It is easier to undress than dress so always start with undressing, e.g. pulling off a T-shirt, unzipping a zip, undoing buttons.

Try this

Learning these skills is not as easy as you might think. Put on a pair of thick gloves and then try to fasten the small buttons on the collar of a shirt. What do you notice? Do you feel frustrated? Do you find yourself using your vision to try to help you locate the button and the hole?

When we cannot 'see' what we are doing we depend upon good feedback from our hands to our brains and body awareness (proprioception – knowing where our body is without using vision). This ability to carry out complex fine motor skills develops with time in typically developing children. Children with Developmental Coordination Disorder (formerly known as Dyspraxia) a condition affecting between 5 and 6% of school-aged children find these skills particularly challenging and may require structured help and support. Increasingly, support from occupational therapists is provided through universal support and school-based intervention (Hutton *et al.* 2016; Missiuna *et al.* 2017). Children with Down syndrome have been found to respond to structured school-based interventions designed to address difficulties with visual processing and perceptual difficulties (Hutton and Patton 2017; Hayton *et al.* 2018).

How do we involve families?

Involving parents and families is a great way to help children make progress in personal independence skills. Why not invite parents to join in with a session you have planned? Give families activities that they can do at home and tell them why it is important for their child to be able to gain these skills. Parents don't need to do formal 'exercises' with their children, but regular practice at the weekend or on holiday can help a child develop.

Where children lack a stable home life or access to support breakfast and after school clubs can provide an opportunity to reinforce these personal self-care activities.

Going to the loo

This section focuses on:

- How children learn to use the toilet and provides information and suggestions about the skills children need to be able to develop independence when using the toilet at school.
- Why establishing good bladder and bowel habits and toilet etiquette at school are an important aspect of a child's early education experience.

Learning how to use the toilet at school is an important part of a child's early experience of education. Developmentally, most children are ready to use the toilet between the ages of 18 months and three years. The expectation is that most children will learn to use the toilet at home and be toilet trained before starting Early Years education. However, an increasing number of children are starting school without these skills or are in the early stages of learning how to control their bladder and bowel (ERIC 2017).

For many children it will be the first time that they will use a toilet away from home. A small number of children may have a medical condition or difficulty that affects their bladder and bowel and ability to use the toilet. If this is the case it is important to involve the family and multidisciplinary team in determining how to manage the child's personal hygiene needs. Early intervention and collaboration between Early Years settings and home can help establish the routines to support toilet training.

Personal independence skills for learning and participation

Many young children in Early Years settings will struggle to balance when sitting on the toilet, find it hard to adjust and fasten their clothing, wipe after using the toilet and wash and dry their hands. Others need help to acquire the habit and routines of using the toilet. Wiping and hand washing every time they use the toilet and learning how to behave, for example, flushing the toilet after use and leaving the toilet clean for other children.

What skills are needed to be able to use the toilet?

- Recognising when the bladder and bowel are full.*
- Being able to sit independently with feet on the floor (see Chapter 3, *Are they sitting comfortably?*).
- Being able to balance when sitting and to reach for the toilet paper and balance while pulling up trousers/pants and adjusting clothing.
- Having good body awareness – knowing where to wipe without looking.
- Being able to manipulate fastenings on clothing, zips, buttons etc.
- Having good hand coordination when opening and closing the toilet door, flushing toilet and washing and drying hands.
- Memorising and sequencing actions, e.g. pull down pants, sit on the toilet, wipe, flush, pull up pants, etc.

* When the bladder is full and needs to empty nerve endings send continuous messages to the brain that the bladder needs to empty. When the bowel is full, in comparison, messages fade if it is not convenient to go to the toilet until such time as it is – for example when seated on the toilet, when the sphincter will relax.

The school environment

Where an infant, junior or primary school is situated in large or complex buildings some children will still be developing their control of their bladder and bowel and often cannot wait for long, once they know that they 'need to go'. Having toilets that are close to the classroom is helpful. If this is not possible, ensuring that the class have regular toilet breaks and time is allocated to enable children to walk to the toilets is essential.

Toilets should be clean, comfortable and safe spaces for children to be in. Privacy is important. Having a door that closes properly and giving children time to visit the toilet should be a priority. The Department of Education have guidance on standards for toilets in schools (Department of Education 2015).

Why are toileting skills important for learning?

Being comfortable

We know that it is important to be comfortable before we can learn or attend. Our basic needs must be met if we are to give our full attention to learning. This includes not being hungry, being comfortable (seating, warmth etc) and having a comfortable bladder and bowel.

Try this

Think of a time or imagine what it would be like if you were at the cinema, concert or lecture and you needed to go to the toilet, but were unable to leave the room. Where would your attention be focused? Would you be able to concentrate on the film, enjoy the concert or listen to the lecture?

When children have difficulty using the toilet

Some children may find using the toilet at school stressful or unpleasant and this may be because they are:

- reacting to unfamiliar noises (sound of a hand dryer);
- smells (strong disinfectants, air freshener); or
- touch (toilet a different height, feel of the seat, wobbly seat).

Some children may dislike visiting the toilet facilities in school and choose to 'hold on' until they return home. 'Hanging on' is not good for children's bladder and bowel health. It is important to be aware when children are having difficulty and to try to identify what the problem is. A good place to start is to visit and check the condition of the Early Years toilets.

Children should also be encouraged to drink water at regular intervals during the day to maintain hydration and encourage a healthy bladder function. A child who does not like using the toilet at school may refuse water to avoid needing to go to the toilet (ERIC 2006, 2019).

Try this

Visit your school/class toilets and check:

- Are the toilets at a reasonable distance from the classroom?
- Are the toilets adequately ventilated and well lit?
- Are the toilets signposted and easy to locate?
- Are the toilets at the right height and is the toilet seat the right circumference for the children in your class?
- Are the toilet seats secure (wobbly toilet seats are often a reason for children not wanting to use the school toilet)?
- Are the toilets and surrounding areas clean?
- Does the flush work on the toilets – is it easy to operate?
- Is there an adequate supply of toilet paper within easy reach of the toilet?
- Can a child easily operate the toilet paper dispenser?
- Can the child close, lock and unlock the door easily?

Finally, ask yourself, would you be happy using the toilet facilities?

Personal independence skills for learning and participation

When teaching children about how to use the toilet think about having a visual poster encourage the children to offer suggestions and create a list of 'Things we do and don't do when using the toilet at school'.

- We always flush the toilet when we have finished using it.
- We always wash and dry our hands.
- We put paper towels in the bin – not on the floor.
- We don't disturb others when they are using the toilet.
- We don't play in the toilet or toilet area.

Bottom cleaning/wiping skills

Many children struggle with cleaning after using the toilet. Children need to be taught to wipe from front to back. It is not unusual for even older children to find this difficult. The reason wiping is difficult is because it involves balancing, reaching backwards and coordinating hands and body without using vision. Children need good body awareness (knowing where their body parts are without looking).

Some activities that encourage development of cleaning/wiping skills are:

- Play games such as passing a ball, balloon or scarf around the body passing from one hand to the other.
- Pass a small ball, balloon or scarf around the legs in a figure of eight.
- Stick stickers on different places on the child's body – front and back and get the child to find the stickers.
- Tuck a scarf into the back of the child's waistband or back pocket and ask them to retrieve it and then replace it.
- Use wet wipes or toilet wipes so that the child can clean themselves more easily.

Summary

This chapter has explored three areas of personal independence that enable young children to build their confidence and be able to participate in Early Years education. We have provided an overview of skills acquisition in typically developing children and explored reasons why some children require additional help when they start in Early Years. Ideas and suggestions have been designed to be incorporated into everyday classroom routines for the benefit all children. Reflect on what you have learnt and consider how you could put into practice ideas presented in this chapter. Can you now answer the questions below?

- Why are independence skills so important to a child's Early Years education?
- Why do some children start Early Years education lacking personal independence skills?
- What might be the benefits to children's education of reviewing Early Years dining and toilet facilities?

Chapter 3: Are they sitting comfortably?

There is truth in the saying 'Are you sitting comfortably? Then we'll begin', as it emphasizes the importance of being comfortable before we can listen. This chapter is about 'good' sitting. We have used the term 'good' loosely to describe a way of sitting that is comfortable for young children, enabling them to be included in the classroom and participate in learning, whether seated on the floor or sitting at a desk. The aim of this chapter is to consider how children develop control of their posture, enabling them to sit independently for longer periods and to think about how we can modify the classroom and school environment to provide comfortable, functional seating for all children, as their bodies develop. Alongside advocating for comfortable seating to be available we also want to avoid prolonged bouts of sitting by creating opportunities for movement throughout the day.

This chapter provides information about:

- The development of postural control in young children.
- How a child's sitting position influences attention and learning.
- Classroom strategies that can promote 'good' sitting in class.
- Ideas about how to change the classroom environment to promote children's comfort and wellbeing when seated.

What do we mean by 'posture and postural control'?

Posture is commonly understood to describe how we sit and stand. Postural control is the control we exert over our postural muscles and balance to achieve functional goals (sitting, standing and moving) within our environment. The development of postural control in childhood therefore involves a dynamic interaction between the child's body and their environment. As a child grows and develops, their body adapts and matures in response to challenges to balance, equilibrium, the pull of gravity and changes in position. Although the major developmental milestones of sitting and walking typically develop in the early years, postural control matures slowly over many years with adult patterns only emerging in late adolescence (Howe and Oldham 2010).

Good postural habits are formed early in life. We know that the child's environment and early movement experiences play a significant role in the development of postural control. Hence comfortable seating in Early Years settings and an awareness of the importance of posture are important contributors to children getting off to a good start.

Maintaining good posture is also important to our own health and wellbeing, helping to prevent back problems and protecting our spine. Back pain during childhood and adolescence influenced by poor sitting habits is not uncommon and can contribute to pain in later life. Evidence that inappropriate school furniture, prolonged sitting in class and carrying heavy school bags causes back pain in children highlights the importance of children building strong back muscles through regular physical activity (United Kingdom, Chief Medical Officer 2019).

Try this

Let's think about our own posture for a moment. Are *you* sitting comfortably?

When we are asked to think about our sitting, we often force ourselves to 'sit up straight', but this isn't necessarily either comfortable or functional – we can't maintain an upright position for long and end up slumping back into a familiar position.

In fact, there isn't one sitting position that is 'good'. Sitting well depends on what we want to do and therefore we need to consider the best position for each task and situation.

How would you describe the 'best' sitting position when completing the following tasks? Think about how upright you need to be and the amount of support you need. Compare your answers to those of other colleagues – how individual do you think are our experiences of 'comfort'?

- Reading a book.
- Writing a letter.
- Eating a meal.
- Watching television.
- Driving a car.
- Ironing.
- Chatting with colleagues.

Check your classroom now and see how many children are sitting 'comfortably', in chairs and at desks that are an appropriate size (refer to the general principles below). Current thinking suggests that achieving a strictly 90-degree angle at the hip, knees and ankles is not necessary and that this should be used only as a general guideline. What is important is for children to be able to place their feet on the floor, or on a stable surface, and to ensure that they are not twisted or tilted in their chairs and that they have a table

that is at a comfortable height (elbows resting on the table top). This is especially important when asking children to carry out more complex fine or precision tasks such as writing (Schneck and Amundson 2010).

What is postural stability and why is it important for learning?

Postural stability is the control we have over our torso, hips and shoulders. The torso is a stable base to which our head and limbs are attached. We can maintain an upright position only by stabilising our torso, enabling us to balance while leaving our hands free to do other things.

When we are sitting in a stable position we can move, turn around, shift our balance forwards or backwards without falling over. We can also steady our neck and head, which is important for us to be able to track moving objects and focus our eyes on objects in the distance. When we ask children to focus their attention on the interactive board in the classroom, look in the direction of the teacher or look at pictures in detail from a book, they will be using their postural muscles and balance to adapt their positioning, stabilize their head and focus their eyes.

When stable, young children are able to free their hands, allowing the skilled and controlled movements required for handwriting, cutting, colouring and all other fine motor or precision skills.

Development of sitting in the young child

The ability to sit unaided usually develops during the first year of life (six to nine months). The child's spine, the muscles surrounding it and the complex postural adjustments required to prevent falling – mature as the child first rolls then sits, crawls and finally walks. What we recognize as the typical 'S' shaped curve of the spine (the curve at the neck and lower back) develops in the early years as the child learns how to resist the force of gravity when holding their head up, controlling their torso and using their arms.

Disruption or delay in the development of postural control can occur because of environmental, social or other individual reasons. It is important to remember that delay or difficulty may be associated with a lack of opportunity for children to move and to 'practise' early movement skills through play.

Try this

Ask children to roll themselves up 'into a ball' whilst laying on their backs with their arms folded on their chest, ask them 'can you roll from side to side?' Then ask them to lie flat on their tummies and stretch out their arms and legs so they are off the floor 'like superman'. Can they hold this position to a count of three to five for young children and five to ten for older children?

Children who find this difficult may also:

- Find it hard to sit without support.
- Use their hands to prop themselves up or hold their head.

- Find it difficult to balance and are often falling off their chair.
- Lack the ability to turn around without losing their balance.

What can we do to help children to a comfortable sitting position?

Think about some of the ideas below that can help all children sit comfortably and may help those who find sitting difficult.

- Check the height of their chair and desk (see previous suggestion) to make sure that they are sitting on furniture that is the right height for them.
- Offer additional back support in their chair or suggest that they sit further back in their chair using the chair to support them.
- When sitting on the floor allow children to lie on their tummy or sit with their back against a wall – positions which provide support and are less tiring than sitting cross-legged.
- Think about your classroom seating plan and check that children are in a good position to see you or the shared teaching resources or board without having to swivel or turn in their chairs.
- Always consult the child to find out what is comfortable and acceptable. Have a range of seating options available for all children to access and use in the classroom.

Why is sitting important to a child's learning?

Young children's bodies are growing and developing, during pre-school, Key Stage 1 and 2 (ages two to 11) and children will change tremendously in terms of their physical development and their ability to maintain an upright and stable posture. Early Years settings need to provide children with a variety of seating and sitting options, which can accommodate the physical changes in height and encourage the habits of good posture early in life.

Children grow and develop at their own pace. In your classroom you will have children who vary in height, weight and size. In pre-school and reception class, children will be moving around the classroom freely and sitting for only short periods of time. However, it is good practice to identify classroom activities such as colouring and drawing, where a task requires precision, coordination and manipulation skills, or when children are expected to sit for longer periods of time such as story time or snack time and check that suitable options for comfortable seating are available.

Try this

Ask the children in your class to line up according to their height and measure the differences between the tallest and shortest in the class. You could incorporate this activity as part of a maths class. Or, ask the children to lie on the floor and draw around one another – pin up the drawings and ask them to measure the differences in height.

What next?

- When arranging your seating plan for the class, mix and match school furniture to include a range of different table and chair heights in your classroom.
- Think about the position of the child who may have more difficulty with balance and sitting, relative to the interactive board and to their neighbours.
- Ask the children themselves to determine what feels comfortable to them.

These suggestions can be implemented for every child in the group or class and so can be considered a universal provision. However, they will assist children with balance or attention needs enabling them to sit still and to be comfortable hence improving their ability to listen to and retain what is being told to them.

'Good' sitting on the floor

During the Early Years education children should be allowed choice in how they sit and encouraged to try out different positions e.g. lying on their tummy, side sitting, sitting with legs stretched out as well as sitting cross-legged. Remind children that they need to be aware of other children around them when they are sitting or lying down. Some young children will find awareness of their own bodies difficult. Ask them to draw an imaginary circle around themselves when they are sitting as their own 'space'.

Encourage children to lie on their tummy and use their elbows to prop their head. This is a good position for children who tire easily when sitting without support. Encourage children to move in and out of different positions. It is unlikely that they will be able to concentrate on a story or listen to instructions if they are uncomfortable.

Sitting cross-legged

Not all children can be expected to sit cross-legged, at least initially, as for many young children this is not a comfortable position or one that they can maintain. Sitting cross-legged does encourage a good hip position so gradually increasing the length of time children sit cross-legged can be a good idea.

Try this

Try sitting cross-legged yourself – notice how tiring this is to maintain for a long period.

- Are you becoming uncomfortable?
- What do you think happens to a child's concentration when they are uncomfortable?

Sitting on a chair at a table for tabletop activities

It is very important when expecting children to carry out tabletop activities to provide good supportive seating and an appropriate sized desk or table. This is because children need to be stable to move their arms and hands freely. The dexterity required to write, for example, requires good upper body and shoulder stability. This applies to writing, drawing, cutting, colouring and using manipulative toys or tools. Share this information with parents and carers so that they can also support their child's development.

Fidgeting is a child's way of indicating that they are tired and/or need to change position. A child who fidgets may have an unsuitable chair or may need additional support. 'Fidget' cushions are sometimes recommended to address issues of fidgeting and attention. These cushions are inflated to create an unstable base which it is thought stimulates the postural muscles and encourages more 'active' sitting. Although there is some evidence to support their use, there is a lack of robust evidence to support their effectiveness as an alternative to traditional classroom seating at present (Seifert and Metz 2017). It is probably better to encourage children to stretch regularly and plan your lessons to include activities that encourage the children to move around the classroom regularly if fidgeting is a problem (Routen *et al.* 2018).

Try this

Try out a 'sitting song' (use the music of a popular nursery rhyme) with children in your class, encourage them to sing before the start of a seated activity or lesson and use signing to reinforce 'good sitting'.

Don't forget to share this sitting song with parents and carers so that they can think about where and how their child sits to colour, draw and read.

'Sitting Song'

Hey, now, everybody sit,
Everybody sit on your chair like this.
Everybody put you bottom right back,
Put your feet flat on the floor.
Everybody now, and then have a stretch and a wiggle,
Then you can learn more.
Hey, now, everybody sit,
Everybody sit on your chair like this.
Everybody sit, everybody sit.

Remember	Tick
Feet flat on the floor	√
Table at a height comfortable to rest arms on table	√
Chair has some back support	√
Consider an angled desktop for writing that enables the forearm to be well supported	√

If you are struggling with inadequate resources bring this to the attention of your Special Educational Needs Coordinator or discuss changing the classroom layout – there may be a low-cost solution that works for your children.

What is the impact of sitting on learning and attention?

A good seated position allows the child to breathe easily, providing oxygen to the brain which will enhance learning and concentration. With the body well supported the child will be more relaxed and able to focus on the task you have set. Good seating enables the head to be positioned symmetrically allowing the eyes to focus properly. Complex cognitive tasks are performed best when children have good support.

Try this

We suggest you try these activities with colleagues. They could be used as part of your in-service training.

- For you to gain an understanding of how challenging it is to carry out complex cognitive tasks when unsupported, try the following:

  Sitting on an exercise ball, (or if you don't have an exercise ball stand on one leg with eyes closed) repeat the eight times table backwards.

- For you to gain an understanding of how hard it is to carry out fine motor skills, when unsupported, try the following: Using the exercise ball (or standing on one leg) try eating cornflakes with chopsticks!

How does classroom design influence learning?

Review your classroom layout with the children.

- On a sheet of squared paper draw out your classroom indicating the position of desks, chairs, resources, wipeboard, lighting etc.
- Consider where you are locating the desks and chairs in relation to the wipeboard.
- Can children see the board easily? Do they have to turn around or swivel in their chairs?
- Try sitting in the chairs and table arrangements you have arranged yourself. Can you see the board? What distractions are present?

- Experiment with different layouts and involve the children in choosing different options. Note any changes in attention, listening and engagement particularly for children who are distractible or have poor attention skills.

Good classroom design can assist children's learning

Design of the classroom has been linked to changes in behaviour in the class and improved learning. If you are expecting children to copy from the board or read from the board it will be much harder for them to maintain good eye and head alignment if they need to turn around. Involving children in decisions about the layout of their classroom can increase their involvement and motivation and provide you with useful feedback. Some teachers may be concerned about loss of authority if they allow children choices about where they sit. When teachers and pupils take decisions together however, they reinforce pupil participation within a healthy school. This exercise, if presented to the children with sufficient information, can provide an opportunity for children to participate in and influence decisions that may assist their learning.

Why do some children have difficulty with sitting and what can you do to help?

When children begin Early Years education, they are expected to be able to sit and maintain attention for longer periods, compared with pre-school. As children progress through the education system, they are expected to sit for longer and longer periods. Older children can spend up to 80% of their school day sitting. There is growing evidence that prolonged sitting contributes to childhood obesity and poor health outcomes (Abbott *et al.* 2013; Mitchell and Byun 2014).

You may observe children who find it difficult to sit for even short periods of time. This can be for a variety of reasons:

- Young children may still be at an early stage of developing their postural muscles and balance responses.
- A child may have a problem making sense of information from the environment, for example being overly sensitive to the texture or 'feel' of the chair, and this may make it hard to sit and listen in class.
- A child who has a disability e.g. Down syndrome, may find it difficult to sit on school furniture because it provides insufficient support. They may need to have an adaptation made to their school chair that provides more support. Always seek advice from a state registered occupational therapist or member of the multidisciplinary team where a child has a recognised disability.

Try this

Observe the children in your class and identify those who:

- Fidget.
- Find it tiring to sit for longer periods.

Consider how you can arrange the classroom to meet children's individual seating needs. Many children do not like to appear 'different' to their peers – how can you make individual adjustments and use additional resources whilst remaining sensitive to the child's need?

Muscle tone is the degree of tension present when muscles are relaxed. Muscle tone varies between individuals. Some of us will have higher 'normal' tone than others. Children with 'low' tone typically find it more difficult to maintain an upright position for longer and tire easily. A typical sign of 'low muscle tone' is when the child slumps or 'drape' themselves over a chair. Children with low tone will often prefer to lie on the floor where there is more support. It can be helpful to use a tool such as the posture observation checklist below to help you find ways to support children who are struggling to sit and attend in the class. The first three questions focus on what is called 'core' stability – the ability to support our head, arms and legs using the core postural muscles of the trunk. The next four questions help you focus on the child's balance. Can they sit on a chair (where there is more support) but not on a bench (with less support)? Does the child's posture alter the longer he/she is expected to sit? The final two questions will help you look in more detail at the chair the child is sitting on. Is it at the correct height so the child can reach the floor with his feet? Is the table at the correct height?

Jot down what you observe and then think about an action plan. When determining an action plan think first about what you can do to change the environment rather than focusing on the child. Can you provide more supportive seating or change your expectation? For example, expect the child to sit for a shorter period/allow the child to sit or lie on the floor. Include opportunities to have frequent rest or movement breaks. Promote opportunities for children to develop their core strength through initiating whole class activities suggested in Chapter 1.

Try this

Consider changing your class routine to include some physical stretching or whole-body activity in between lessons.

Warm up activities prior to sitting in class can help increase muscle tone by stimulating the postural muscles to work harder. Try out some of the warm-ups suggested below. Allow the children a little time to cool down before the start of a sitting activity in class.

- Ten x jumping on the spot.
- Ten x star jumps.
- Ten x spotty dog (spotty dog is where the child's opposite hand and leg moves alternately).

If time allows, vary your activities perhaps use a parachute activity with the children – for example tossing a ball in the air and catching it in the parachute,

Table 3.1 Posture Observation Checklist

['he' and 'his' will be used throughout this checklist for ease of writing]

Name of pupil: D.o.b: Class:

Can the child …	Yes	No	Comments	Action
lay on his back with arms folded on his chest and roll up 'into a ball'?				
lay on his back and roll from side to side?				
lie on his tummy and stretch out his arms and legs so that they are off the floor (like Superman) and hold this position for five seconds?				
sit on a chair or on the floor without any support (e.g. arms/wall/floor) for his back?				
sit on a chair without falling off it?				
sit on a bench without falling off it?				
turn around (when standing or sitting) without losing balance?				
sit comfortably on his chair with feet flat on the ground?				
rest his arms comfortably on his desk (with a straight back)?				

roll the ball around within the parachute. This activity is excellent for encouraging shoulder strength. If you try holding the parachute yourself you will be able to 'feel' your shoulder muscles working hard against gravity, this happens when you are doing any activity that involves holding your arms in the air.

Summary

This chapter has covered the topic of sitting and seating in the Early Years settings. We have considered how postural control develops in young children and how important it is that young children are provided with appropriate and comfortable seating options.

Reflect on what you have learnt and consider how you could implement some of the suggestions into your classroom routines or daily practice. Can you answer the following questions?

Is there a single sitting position that we can describe as good?
What is a common cause of fidgeting in young children?
What type of learning activities require children to be in a comfortable seated position with feet flat on the floor?
Can you identify two modifications to the classroom layout that can improve the learning environment?

Chapter 4: Confident handwriting

Despite all of the technological advances in recent decades handwriting continues to be considered an important form of communication for children. Parents and carers in western societies still expect their children to be able to produce a neat and legible piece of handwriting within a given time frame. This social expectation starts to develop very early on for many young children (two or three years old), as they are encouraged to 'write' their name on cards to family members, which undoubtedly, gives the recipient lots of pleasure. In return, the children receive praise and attention, creating a positive feeling for them and motivating them to keep producing handwriting.

As children get older the school system continues to consider handwriting an essential life skill with children in primary and secondary schools still required to carry out tasks requiring handwriting for an average of between 30 and 60% a day (Blythe 2015). Of course, handwriting in schools is also utilised as a means to assess knowledge and understanding (for the majority of children and young people) in examinations. Displays on school boards also frequently show case not only well written and thought-provoking stories and understanding, but also every child's 'best handwriting.' However, not every child finds handwriting easy, and if they don't have the opportunity to learn and practise in a supportive environment it can become a task to be avoided and can impact negatively on their self-esteem, confidence and academic engagement.

Think back to how many times someone close to you praised you (or not) for your handwriting. How did they describe your writing? Did they use language like 'lovely', 'neat' or words which are not so positive? How did this make you feel? Now think about which children you work with who enjoy mark making or writing, or not?

This section will provide information about:

- The complexities of the handwriting task.
- The developmental stages of handwriting.
- Pencil grip.
- The left-handed writer.
- A whole nursery/school approach to handwriting – policy and practice.
- Classroom strategies to help develop efficient handwriting skills.

Handwriting is a complex task

When asked what is involved in producing a handwritten script the most straightforward answer could be to describe it as a fine motor skill. In reality however, it is far from this simple …

In recent years, with our daily use of technology ever increasing I have on a number of occasions heard colleagues and friends, when asked to complete a handwritten task, say how strange it feels to write and how messy their handwriting has become. They become uncomfortable using a pen or pencil to produce information for others to read and will try to hand this task to another or revert to typing. With this in mind let's think for a moment about what is involved when we write.

Try this

The task: pick up a pen or pencil and write a sentence

Now, reflect for a moment on what you have just done – what was involved as you followed that deceptively simple instruction 'to write something'? What skills and abilities did you draw on? Did your environment enable you to carry out the task successfully?

Your first thought was possibly '*what shall I write*'? Having an idea and wanting to express this is an important precursor to writing. Appreciating this helps us understand how important it is for children to actually have something they want to write about and that they want to communicate their ideas, as well as their knowledge and understanding, through mark making, drawing and writing.

As you decided what to write you were focusing all your attention, for that moment, on the process of writing. To help you appreciate how important the ability to *concentrate* is to be able to write, try making the decision about what to write about whilst watching television or having a conversation with someone! Was it as easy as you perhaps initially thought it would be?

Once you had decided what to write you picked up a pen or pencil and *grasped* it in your *preferred hand*. You needed to be able to *control the movement* of the pen sufficiently to make recognisable marks. Feedback from your fingers helped your *sensory system* understand exactly how much force to apply to the pen as you wrote. Your *other hand automatically steadied* the paper. You probably adjusted *your sitting position* so your head was supported, and your *eyes* could read what you had written.

As you wrote your sentence your brain was simultaneously carrying out a *cognitive task* – enabling you to create complex symbols (letters made of shapes) based on sounds into a series of meaningful words …

And you carried out all these highly complex skills quickly and 'without thinking.' Return to the words in italics above. What do they tell you about the complexities of handwriting? For a young child to be able to write they need to have something they want to communicate to others about. They need to be able to concentrate on this one task for a period of time and to think about how and what needs to be written. Then of course they need to have the motor, coordination and sensory skills necessary to hold a pencil or crayon efficiently, to sit comfortably and to form letters and numbers. Look at all the skills young children need to develop and practise before they even pick up a pencil to write!

Getting ready for handwriting

Handwriting skills need to be experienced, learnt and practised stage by stage and details of these stages are discussed later on in this section. This is especially important to remember in the United Kingdom because of the age (four or five years old) children start formal education. Remember, handwriting is not fully physically secure until a typically developing child reaches the age of ten (Blythe 2015).

To reach the required handwriting level of producing a legible script a child must move through each development stage and if this is rushed or a child is expected to move onto a stage before mastering an earlier one, long-term problems are likely to hinder the child's success as a writer. Also, it is important that young children avoid learning inefficient and incorrect letter formations. This is because handwriting is partly a motor skill and if letter formations are practised, incorrectly, they nevertheless still become permanent in children's motor memories. As we all know reversing a learnt motor skill is difficult!

Try this

Imagine you have started dancing classes with a friend. The third week you go the times of the different classes have been altered without prior notice. You find yourself in the advanced class expected to perform a perfect tango. You watch the others in the group and try to copy. You can't keep up and although you master the odd move everything around you is going too fast and your anxiety at looking a little foolish isn't helping your performance either. It seems obvious that you should go back to the beginners' dancing class to securely learn the basics – and then one day you will also be able to tango!

Don't rush a child and be sure that every child is developmentally ready to write when you start this work.

The importance of motor and sensory skills for the development of handwriting

We are sure you will not be surprised to know that the development of gross motor skills is needed to enable a child to hold a pencil. Large shoulder and arm pattern movements with crayons, paint or just in the air are really positive activities to encourage. There are a number of programmes available on the market which focus on helping develop gross motor movements.

Physical activities such as crawling also helps a child build and develop strength in their shoulders and wrists, as well as hand/eye coordination. 'Good sitting' is another crucial factor in this process because without being able to sit in a stable/balanced way (without having to pay attention to achieving this) a child will not have the cognitive space to focus on listening and learning. For this reason, it is essential that young children's feet (whole of foot, not just the toes) are always able to touch the ground (see Chapter 3 for information about positive sitting).

As well as gross motor skills, early *play* opportunities help child to use their hands and fingers to manipulate objects and to feel different textures. Such play is the start of the development of fine motor skills. Alongside manipulative play, games which require being able to recognise different shapes such as snap and spot the difference provide children opportunities to practise *visual skills*. Children are then encouraged to colour, to scribble and then to trace using a pencil over patterns and to do 'join the dots' activities.

Check that before you ask a child to start learning to write they can

1. Sit in a stable/balanced way on a chair or stool (with both feet firmly on the ground).
2. Pick up and release objects with accuracy.
3. Use their hands together. One hand needs to be the 'doer' hand and the other a 'helper' hand.
4. Coordinate the handwriting skill well enough between their eyes and hands.
5. Attend for long enough to ENJOY the mark making process and are MOTIVATED to want to use a pencil.

First signs of mark making

In terms of dexterity and precision skills the child's ability to carry out the precise movements required to draw shapes begins early in life with the emergence of larger 'gross' movement patterns. This is why opportunities to build confidence in children's large movement skills are so important in the Early Years (see earlier section on Movement and Learning) (Strauss n.d.).

We can observe the developmental progression that occurs from larger movement patterns to small precise movements through observing the development of 'pencil grasp' in young children. For example, a toddler given a thick crayon will grasp this crudely with their whole hand (cylindrical grasp 12–15 months). They will swap hands freely while they create large sweeping and spontaneous 'patterns' that involve their whole body. As the child matures they begin to exercise greater control over their body and posture, enabling them to make, still crude, but now deliberate marks with the crayon. The emergence of a 'preferred' hand will enable the part of their brain responsible for motor learning, to specialise, in turn making precise skills easier and more automatic. Alongside a maturing grasp and the ability to exercise greater control over their movement patterns, the child will exercise other choices, over colour, shape and form. As children's creative imagination develops, their drawing and painting and mark making skills will emerge alongside a maturing grasp.

The following is considered the most typical development of mark making and pre-writing skills:

1. Random scribbles and marks.
2. Horizontal scribbles.
3. Vertical scribbles.
4. Circular scribbles.

Then as children begin to learn to integrate cognitive, perceptual and motor skills the pre-writing shapes needed for letter formation begin to emerge. There is a growing consensus that once the foundation of skills of writing are achieved (e.g. able to sit, attend, dexterity etc) the most effective approaches focus on practising letter formation and writing to communicate.

Pencil grips

As a child's whole body becomes more stable (e.g. trunk, shoulders, elbows, wrist and knuckle joints) movements needed to form letters become more precise and focused on the distal (furthest away from the body) joints of the fingers, especially the index finger and thumb. Do note that it is quite usual for children right up until the end of Key Stage 1 to use their whole arm when writing. As the need for this whole arm movement decreases (more stable) then the child's handwriting will become more fluent and neater. The typical stage of pencil grip (or grasp) development is:

A cylindrical grip

This begins to emerge between the age of one and 1.5 years. The crayon/pencil is held with the fist with a slightly flexed wrist. You will notice that with a cylindrical grip the child's arm moves as one unit.

A digital grip

At this stage (two to three years old) the child holds the writing tool with their fingers. The wrist is straight, and the hand is facing downwards (pronated). By now only the forearm moves as one unit.

A modified tripod grip

As the child develops their handwriting skills, they will move to what is called a static modified tripod grip. At this stage only the hand moves as one unit, the ring and little finger are slightly flexed, and the child's fingers are moved back from the tip of the pencil or crayon.

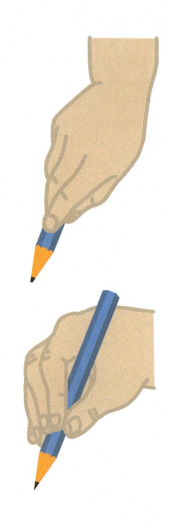

A tripod grip

At this final stage a child develops a dynamic tripod grip when the ring and little fingers are flexed, knuckles are stable and there is only slight wrist extension.

The current thinking is that the child's actual type of grip is not as important as it was once thought, as long as it is efficient, legible and does not cause pain, tiredness or block the location and view of the writing.

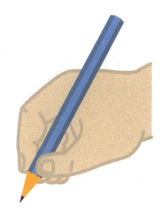

What to do when a child is having difficulty holding a pencil

Sometimes the small joints of the hand are not sufficiently stable for efficient handwriting. Hyperextension of the small distal joints in the fingers may occur in some instances. This can mean that the child applies too much pressure in an attempt to stabilise the pencil. This can cause pain and discomfort and the additional effort required can lead to tiredness and fatigue. If this continues without support it

can lead to a lack of motivation to write and lowered self-esteem. Think about modifying your expectations of the length of time children who have this difficulty are expected to write without a break. Use of a soft pencil or roller pen can help so that children don't need to apply additional pressure, appropriate stable seating and frequent rest breaks can help children develop a functional grip.

Try this

1. Observe a child who you consider has a poor or immature pencil grip. Can you see that the movements the child carries out to form letters come from the arm and or wrist and not the fingers?
2. Now try to write for a period of between ten and 15 minutes without stopping, using your non-writing hand. What does your hand/fingers feel like? Do you ache anywhere? What does your handwriting look like?

By doing this you hopefully can begin to understand how important it is for young children to develop an efficient pencil grip as soon as they are physically able. If not achieved before the beginning of Key Stage 2 when writing becomes an important part of a school day, they can lose motivation to write, develop strategies to avoid writing, experience low self-esteem and disengage with learning.

A note about colouring

Do the children you work with move the piece of paper around to colour in? Why do children do this?

By the time children are ready to join Key Stage 2 they should be able to colour quite accurately. They should also be able to colour in without moving the piece of paper around. If they can't it could be that they are only using horizontal strokes and therefore move the paper rather than their hand. To be able to colour a whole picture without moving the paper children need to be able to use multiple angles and strokes. Using multiple angles and strokes is also essential for the development of a fluent and legible cursive handwriting script.

Supporting the child's journey from mark making to writing

As we have discussed throughout this book children's developmental progress follows a typical sequence, but occurs at a different pace for every child. The development of writing is no different to the development of walking or speech. Each child will achieve these 'milestones' in their own way and the influence of their environment plays an important role in how they achieve these steps.

Supporting children's journey from mark making to writing requires Early Years settings to adopt a truly holistic approach and this is probably the single most influential factor in promoting the development of writing. Think back to the earlier exercise – how hard was it for you to 'untangle' the differing aspects of motor, cognitive and motivational aspects at work as you wrote your sentence?

The Early Years environment needs to stimulate all the child's senses and to encourage development across the motor, cognitive and emotional domains. Children will be at different stages in their development when they start Early Years education. Some will be eager to pick up a crayon or pencil and will be colouring in and starting to make meaningful drawings and recognisable letter shapes. Others will be less confident and would rather be playing with toys rather than colouring or drawing. We know many children will start Early Years education lacking the foundational or fundamental motor skills required. Those working in Early Years can stimulate the development of these skills by following these three simple principles to create a 'writing ready' environment:

- Holistic and whole class – create an environment that stimulates all the child's senses.
- Fun and playful – maintain motivation and interest of children as they start their writing journey by choosing fun and playful activities.
- Developmental awareness – 'Go backwards to move forwards' if children are struggling. Underpin your practice through greater appreciation of how young children develop the skills to write.

Creating an Early Years 'writing ready' environment

Here are some pointers to help you think about and create your own Early Years 'writing ready' environment.

- Do you have a rich and varied variety of mark making 'tools' for children to experiment with and enjoy? Attractive crayons, pencils, pens and chalks that are an appropriate size (less than 10cm long and 1–2 cm wide) and sturdy enough for small hands to grasp?

- Do you have a range of different types of paper and other material that includes different colours and textures that the child can use to make marks alongside good quality writing paper? Build up a resource of silver foil, wallpaper, wrapping paper etc.
- Are your pencils and crayons sharpened regularly and are they easy to use? Give children the responsibility of finding pencils that need sharpening. Choose 'soft' chalks and pencils and crayons that make a mark easily without the child having to press hard on the paper. Throw away old materials.
- Are your pencils and crayons and other mark making resources accessible for children? Are they on view and attractively presented? Are they positioned so that children can reach them easily?
- Have you checked your tables and chairs and made sure they are the correct height and size for *all* children in your class?
- Can children see the interactive board from where they are sitting without having to turn around or twist in their chairs?
- Have you a 'mark making' corner in your classroom with resources readily to hand where children can spend time enjoying drawing and mark making?
- Children learn best when they are enjoying an activity. Choose a 'just right' writing challenge which will help to maintain a child's motivation. This is a challenge that encourages the child to achieve a goal and then go 'just beyond' the limit of their capacity, helping them to build confidence and self-esteem.
- If a child is struggling with a writing task – you may need to take a 'step back' or consolidate an earlier skill, before the child can confidently 'go forward'. This approach is relevant to Early Years where children will be at differing developmental stages. Many children will enjoy and benefit from continuing to engage in some pre-writing activities, for example, messy play and large mark making activities that involve the child's whole body.
- Do you have a range of motivating and playful activities that encourage children to explore the early stages of writing? Remember that we write to communicate? Drawing on children's imaginative world can help to motivate children who may be reluctant to start to write?
- Think about how you can provide constructive, positive feedback and encouragement for children? Do you have somewhere to exhibit children's work? Do you build in time to reward effort?
- The outdoor environment is just as important as the classroom when building skills for writing. Children's outdoor play encourages the development of gross motor skills, confidence and self-esteem.
- Involve parents and carers by inviting children to bring examples of drawing and writing from home, and send home examples of their school work.

Try this

Choose a pencil that hasn't been sharpened for a while and a felt tip pen that is running out of ink. Try writing out the sentence '*The quick brown fox jumps over the lazy dog*' several times. Try again writing with an oversized pencil (at least 30cm in length!). How do you feel? Do you want to give up? What about the quality of your writing?

This exercise provides a useful insight into the importance of having writing tools that are appropriately designed for, and the correct size for, children to hold, use and enjoy.

The left-handed writer

Being a child who writes (and carries out other activities) using their left hand can be confusing and difficult. Teachers need to think about the environment, activities and equipment from a left-handed writer's point of view. Of course, young children may not have decided what hand is their preferred dominant hand and so placing tools to the centre should be maintained. When a child's hand dominance is secure then it is important that you ensure left-handed children gain the specific knowledge to help them achieve and develop in what is often a right-hander's environment. This also includes making sure that there is immediate access to appropriate equipment such as left-handed scissors and measuring materials. The location of a child's seating position within the classroom and positioning of tools such as a computer mouse is important to encourage engagement and success.

Think about

1. Seating position

- This is often forgotten within a busy classroom, but it is so important that left-handed writers sit at the left-hand end/edge of a table or desk. This gives them space to move their left arm and also prevents their writing hand from knocking against another child (and then being told off for annoying another child).
- *Secondly*, don't forget about lighting (daylight and artificial). Try to make sure that the light comes from the right side of the child.
- *Thirdly*, (as long as their feet can still touch the ground) give them a slightly higher chair so that they can get a better view of their work and also it will release their forearm.

2. Paper position

- This is such an easy strategy to use to support the left-handed writer, and it can really make a difference if introduced to the child when they first begin to write. Angle the paper to the right just a small amount (about 8 degrees) ensuring that the child can still see the words they have just written.

3. Pencil grip and letter formation

- If the positioning of the paper to the right becomes part of the writing process early on for a left-hander this should help avoid the child rotating and straining their wrist inwards to write. A child will do this so that they can see what they have written, but of course this positioning of the wrist can make the child alter their seating posture and thus may impact on their hand–eye coordination and cause back or neck discomfort. Therefore, make sure that the child has their hand below the line.

Also, a pencil should not be held too close to the end (between 2 and 3cm) so that it helps them to see what they have written.

- Another factor to remember is that a left-handed child will *push* their pencil as they write. A right-handed child will *pull* a pencil. Therefore, to help the pencil smoothly across the page a left-handed writer will require a pencil which isn't too sharp.
- A left-handed child will also often cross 'f' and 't' from the right to the left and so they will find it is easier not to join these two letters.

4. Classroom equipment and tools

- Left-handed scissors in every classroom is essential to enable a left-handed child to cut with skill. Left-handed scissor blades are reversed allowing the user to produce a clean rather than an uneven cut.
- Ensure that other tools such as a computer mouse have enough flex/space to enable them to be positioned either to the right or left of the computer.
- Rulers/clocks. It is possible to purchase left-handed rulers and other pieces of equipment such as clocks. However, it is important to remember that left-handed children will need to be prepared to live in what is a right-handed world and therefore encouraging reading words and numbers from left to right and to read a clock clockwise. This can be supported by marking with a coloured dot 'starting' points in books or a bold number **1**.

Try this

If you are a right-handed person you may not recognise the challenges or perhaps adaptations left-handed people need to make on a daily basis. Go into your kitchen at home and look at the cooking equipment you have.

Can your measuring jug be read if you hold it in your right and left hand?

Can the bread board be used for a left-handed person or is it in a space where they cannot use the bread knife efficiently?

What about the positioning of cupboard handles? Are they on the left-hand side and so open to the right? Note how difficult it is to open these doors with your left hand.

If you have ever purchased a takeaway mug of drink from with a shop do you notice where some assistants write your name (for collection)? It is usually on the left of the mug ...

Is your vegetable peeler able to be used by both left- and right-handed people?

As you perhaps can imagine a young child who has a dominant left hand may need longer to learn new tasks and skills which due to space or convention require them to ask their brain to send messages along their non-dominant side. This will require time and practise (and patience and understanding from adults and peers). Handwriting is undoubtedly one of these skills and so ensuring children have the most efficient seat and paper positioning and pencil grip can make a real difference to their development.

Confident handwriting

How should handwriting be taught?

Individual letters first?

Nationally there is currently no clear guidance from the Department for Education (DfE) about *how* handwriting should be taught. For example, current national guidance says that acquiring accurate and appropriate letter shape, size and spacing should be emphasised before joins are taught. However, it also implies that a casual cursive style should be used. This means that it is recognised that there are certain letters when adjacent to another that are best left without a join (un-joined). Thus, many teachers, believe that it is better to teach letter forms that are as simple as possible, perhaps using an approach such as 'formation families' (Hulme undated) which also reflect the writing in texts children are going to be accessing on a daily basis. Joining, if and when deemed appropriate for each child can be achieved using exit strokes only. Andrea Webb (former chair of the National Handwriting Association, https://nha-handwriting.org.uk) (Webb undated) presents an argument for children to be introduced to handwriting by using a separate letter font such as Sassoon font. Using theory and research to support her argument (such as MacArthur *et al.* 2006) she also provides examples of observations some teachers made about children and adults handwriting:

1. The majority of adults do not write fully cursively; most use a mix of joined and un-joined script.
2. Many adolescents who have been taught joined script in the primary school abandon it when they get to secondary school in order to achieve greater speed when the demands of the curriculum increase.
3. Un-joined script may retain legibility for longer when handwriting speed increases, as in exams.
4. Forcing children with motor coordination difficulties to join may create a range of unnecessary problems with writing and result in an aversion to doing it. It is possible to achieve a stylish, functional, fluent joined or part-joined script without using the 'Continuous Cursive' model.
5. Whilst anecdotal evidence suggests that handwriting supports spelling (e.g. Cripps 1995), there is no evidence that this applies only to writing in cursive styles of script.

(https://nha-handwriting.org.uk/handwriting/articles/continuous-cursive-cure-or-curse/)

Try this

Ask all the teachers in your school to provide you with a standard sample of their handwriting within a five-minute period. Which do you think is the most legible and stylish? Does it remain the same or become less readable as the end of the five minutes approaches? Do your findings align/disagree with Andrea Webb's findings?

Cursive script

In contrast to the 'individual letter first' approach however there are practitioners who consider that 'lead in strokes' and 'exit strokes' i.e. fully cursive writing, should be taught from the start of formal education in line with many other European countries. So, are there any cautionary factors to be considered prior to making this whole school decision? We would suggest that there two main factors that need to be discussed before any decisions are made. Firstly, and very pragmatically, formal writing in many other European countries is not introduced until children are around seven years of age, whilst in the UK it is between four and five years of age. Secondly, as has been mentioned throughout this chapter, handwriting is a complex developmental perceptual motor skill and as such new skills (cognitive, perceptual and motor) can only be learnt when children are mature enough to be able to integrate them. Such developmental factors suggest that as a universal approach this could still be appropriate for implementation in schools in the UK. However, it could be said to be an inclusion concern as children who have a special educational need or/and disability or are vulnerable due to early life experiences, may not have reached this developmental stage by the time they are four or five. They will therefore be asked and expected to be successful at producing cursive script when they are not developmentally ready. As you will be fully aware this can very easily lead children to feel frustrated or upset that they can't achieve what is being asked of them. Such responses can lead to behaviour issues, anxiety, stress and a disengagement with learning very early in their school life. Not all agree with this view such as Montgomery (2007) who believes it is helpful to teach full cursive writing from the beginning. Thus, although we are focusing on the importance of universal provision and outcomes in this book, it is of course crucial that any impact on all children is vital to consider and should be part of your overall approach to inclusive practice.

The importance of practice

Within the last decade, research studies have found that it is essential for all children to have regular practice in handwriting in order to improve letter formation quality, speed and legibility (Hoy *et al.* 2011) over a period of time. Such an approach to learning handwriting is consistent with the theory of motor learning (Zwicker and Harris 2009: 302). As improvements in handwriting are seen with regular practice for the majority it is quite likely that children become more motivated to keep practising their handwriting and therefore value it as an activity. Conversely, it has also been found that if a child is asked to move on too quickly having failed to master the basics of letter formation then it is quite likely that they will experience handwriting problems later on and try to avoid this activity!

Fortunately, although the National Curriculum does not require schools to practise handwriting most schools do see the value in this activity. Some may practise on a daily basis, but with the highly demanding curriculum this is not always possible. Even if you can only practise twice or three times a week it is important to remember that teachers and all educators need to observe the children to ensure that their posture, pencil grip, letter formation and placement are all evidencing good practice. There are many ways to help with this for a whole class such as the song introduced in Chapter 3.

We therefore think that it is important that an Early Years setting or school develops a handwriting policy which takes into consideration the stages of development children will go through in the process of learning how to write, the type of script to be adopted and how a consistent message is going to be shared across the school.

The importance of a handwriting policy

One thing that can be extremely helpful for all children is a consistent approach to handwriting throughout their Early Years' education (and indeed later). There is nothing more confusing for a child to learn one way of writing one academic year and then be told they have to 'unlearn' this when they start in the next class. Additionally, adults in classrooms might have very different writing styles and therefore the modelling of handwriting on whiteboards and presentation boards can again cause confusion for children. It is for these reasons that we recommend every Early Years setting should have a handwriting policy which everyone follows. If at all possible it would be in the children's best interest to also collaborate between perhaps a nursery setting and a school so that even if the children are still only at the pre-writing pattern stage when they move provision what they see modelled by adults and on screens or presentations is once again consistent. I expect you can imagine how this might be reassuring, especially for those children who lack confidence or are already experiencing motor skill issues.

Try this

Firstly, copy a paragraph of writing in your first language and see how the end result makes you feel. Now copy a paragraph of unfamiliar written script, perhaps Arabic. What difficulties do you experience with regards to legibility, speed and understanding? How would you feel if you were asked to read the Arabic letters or abjad (alphabet) aloud to your peers? Can you see how this might be a similar experience for young children who are expected to understand different styles of handwriting from one year to the next?

A whole nursery and school approach to handwriting

I hope you are now very aware of how important it is for children, and young children in particular, to be taught how to write using a consistent approach which recognises the stages of development rather than the age of the children. We feel that one way to achieve this is to establish and embed a handwriting policy across the whole setting or school.

Think about the following questions:

- Has your Early Years setting got a handwriting policy?
- Do you know what handwriting style your Early Years providers or feeder schools follow?

Then think about what you would need to do before you can write a policy. For example:

- Do an audit of the styles of handwriting staff use in your setting.
- Decide whether you are going to teach children how to form letters using cursive or print script. Take advice or undertake your own research about the strengths and limitations of using either a cursive or print script in Early Years education. Refer to the section about the use of different scripts.
- Consult with your local schools or Early Years settings about what style of handwriting they promote.
- Engage with parents and carers about their thoughts on handwriting styles.
- Think about possible training needs of staff and parents (and the budget required to do this).
- Think about whether you will need different resources, such as a computer programme, new wooden/plastic letters etc.
- Think about the classroom environment. How do you organise the furniture and where is the whiteboard if children need to read or copy any form of mark making? Is the lighting sufficient and do you have blinds/curtains to block out strong light or reflections?

I am sure there are other factors you feel you also need to consider, but the issues mentioned above will give you a good start.

A whole school handwriting policy will need to be written to meet the needs of your specific community, but the headings in Table 4.1 might help you get started.

Table 4.1 An example of a Handwriting Policy Template

A whole nursery/school handwriting policy template (example only)

Aims:
The role of parents and carers:
Adults' handwriting in the nursery/school:
Inclusion: equal/equity of opportunities
Knowledge, skills and understanding:
Stages of handwriting development

- Nursery/Early Years
- End of the Foundation Stage:
- Year One
- Year Two
- Year Three and beyond

Teaching and learning:

- The style of handwriting to be used throughout the nursery/school
- Assessment
- The use of ICT

Resources: Whole school resources/classroom based/specialist intervention/equipment
The basic format of a handwriting lesson:

The following is a case study from a 0–19 Academy. It clearly shows what can be achieved by the implementation of a whole school policy where a consistent approach to handwriting is followed.

> **Case Study 4.1**
>
> ***Handwriting Case Study (Primary Years)***
>
> Having a whole school handwriting policy has enabled the Academy to focus on developing well-presented, fluent and legible handwriting. The Academy chose to implement a cursive handwriting script. This has meant that all PowerPoint presentations, writing on boards, display writing and the modelling of handwriting by staff is done using cursive script. This consistent approach has led to the increased ability of pupils to both read and develop their own cursive writing style. It is felt that this consistent approach is key to pupils' handwriting progress. This approach also includes regular class teacher and parent reviews of pupils' progress during which success can be celebrated and new targets or objectives set together.

Universal/whole class strategies

Firstly, it is important to say that we have found regular practice for every child is crucial for the development of handwriting. Pupils in all classes can access pencil grips or triangular pencils/pens to support them in the development of an efficient, comfortable pencil grip and this can make an immediate positive impact. Grips and triangular pencils also help those pupils whose hands tire quickly due to a tight pencil grip. By using a pencil grip/triangular pencil (a design of their choice) pupils can achieve a greater writing speed with improved letter formation resulting in less tired fingers and hands. Sloping boards are also freely available in classes when pupils feel they need additional help with their posture when writing. Manufacturers are now producing equipment such as cutlery, pens and pencils ergonomically designed for little hands. *[NOTE: A word of caution about introducing any adapted writing equipment. It is very important that there is a good understanding about why they are being used, how they work/may help and that the child is comfortable using them].*

Targeted handwriting interventions

In Reception and Y1, pupils identified as struggling with writing are identified and placed into fine motor skills targeted (short-term) small intervention groups (up to five pupils), run by a teaching assistant twice a week (20 minutes each session). The activities are aimed at developing hand and finger muscle control and include using play dough, pegs, cutting activities using scissors, colouring, handwriting sheets, finger rhymes and songs. Pupils also access a gross motor skills group. Importantly, pupil progress is reviewed and recorded at the end of each session by the teaching assistant and monitored weekly by the class teacher. For some pupils a six-week intervention programme is sufficient for progress to be made, whilst others may continue with the group into the following term. Additionally, the class teacher and Special Educational Needs Coordinator (SENCO) consider each child's development in all other areas and identify other possible links to the lack of progress, including language delay, processing difficulties or possible developmental delay.

Self-esteem

As pupils see their handwriting become more legible and well-formed, their self-esteem and motivation also improves. The pupils become keen to write, and their engagement in learning improves. Adult praise and encouragement then further grow the pupils' self-esteem and motivation. Pupils positively beam with happiness and display a sense of improved confidence in their abilities which leads them to strive further with their work. Often this is displayed by pupils producing more writing and at a greater speed. Pupils' have told us:

> 'I like writing and I'm able to join my letters. I think my handwriting looks nice.'
> 'I can join up my letters and I like to join up as it's easier and it looks better.'
> 'My writing is neat, and I can read it easily. I take my time with my writing. I'm pleased my handwriting looks so nice, especially when I join up.'
> 'I enjoy writing, because I love writing and getting all my stories ideas down.'
> 'I like writing now, because I can write more easily, and I can write much more than before.'

All pupils enjoy the tasks and try hard, despite the initial challenges.

Parental involvement

Parental involvement is also extremely valuable in supporting handwriting. Over half the children who have accessed the fine motor skills interventions to date were also found to have difficulties with self-care skills involving their hands, such as managing zips and buttons and eating with a knife and fork. Therefore, it is important that parents are also encouraged to practise life skills on a daily basis at home.

(written by Mrs H. Ahmet, SENCO, Primary Years, The John Wallis C of E Academy, Ashford, Kent)

What if a child continues to have difficulties?

If a child continues to have difficulty in developing a legible and flowing script despite being provided with a rich and enjoyable early writing environment then it will be important to observe the child's mark making and/or handwriting to identify where difficulties are occurring. Don't forget to record your thoughts and interventions in writing – just in case you need them in the future. Questions to ask could be:

- At what level is the child functioning developmentally? (e.g. What is their grip like? Are they still using their whole body to write?) Re-read the sections about developmental stages to help you think about this.
- What skills do the child need to improve? How can you help them do this?

At the same time as doing these things you can help the child with a few strategies which will help compensate for their difficulties. These could include:

- Using triangular pencils and crayons (to help improve the child's grasp).
- Using rubber pencil grips (to help improve the child's grasp).

- Using a finger spacer to help them leave spaces between words (to help the child understand that words are a form of communication and need to follow rules).
- Using a large dot at the point where the child needs to start to write and another dot (in another colour) showing where the line of writing should stop.
- Squared paper (in maths) and lines for other writing to help improve the organisation of any writing, including the size of the print.

> Don't forget to involve the child's parents in all these discussions because they can help by continuing to practise fun activities at home with the child.

By providing support at the developmental functioning level of the child alongside providing compensatory strategies as well, it is quite likely you and the child will begin to see steady improvements in their handwriting (McMurray *et al.* 2009). If you see no improvement and the impact on the child is beginning to affect their self-esteem, motivation and/or self-confidence, then seek further advice and help from a member of the multidisciplinary team.

Summary

In this chapter we have looked at how we can help children achieve a confident handwriting style which is legible, well-formed and achieved in a timely fashion. The complexity of the task of handwriting is clearly described and considered, with some 'try this' activities to help us recall how difficult writing actually is. The stages of handwriting development are then explained with additional information about being a left-handed writer. A short discussion about the different approaches to handwriting (cursive script or not) is also included, before the importance of a whole Early Years and school approach and policy for handwriting are introduced. Most importantly I hope this chapter has shown how handwriting cannot be left just to chance and its significance for children's academic experiences, self-esteem, confidence and motivation to learn.

Chapter 5: Working together with parents and carers
Signposting ideas for home

This book has explored Early Years settings with a focus on practical suggestions and ideas for practitioners who want to support young children develop the skills they need to participate and learn. This final section acknowledges the significance of 'home' in a child's life and the importance of Early Years practitioners and parents working together. Home should be a safe place for children with parents and other family members providing support and encouragement as the child develops, but we need to acknowledge that this is not the case for all children. Vulnerable children, those in care and children in receipt of pupil premium may have a different experience of home. Many children live in homes that lack basic amenities or are in families that are unable to establish, for many reasons, the routine and structure that young children need to develop independence skills. In the UK, 30% of children are living in poverty equating to nine children in a classroom of 30 (Department of Works and Pensions 2019). Early Years settings can play a significant role in addressing inequalities providing opportunities for children to catch up and overcome disadvantage. Early Years practitioners and others working with young children are often well placed to offer advice and signpost families to sources of advice and support. Actively encouraging and involving parents and carers in some of the activities associated with learning and independence that we have covered in this book can also break down barriers. Both parents and Early Years settings can contribute – parents can reinforce and build on the child's strengths at school and Early Years settings can celebrate and value what children achieve outside of school.

Utilising the influence of parent governors, ensuring that information is updated on the Early Years website and including information in newsletters to parents are some of the ways that schools and Early Years settings can engage and involve parents.

Try this

Do you know what children are doing at home? What are their interests and how are they spending their time? Take some time to find out what children's interests are and what they love doing (e.g. are they part of a club or do they play a particular sport?). Make a record of this and find time to allow all of the children to talk about/show what they are good at or love participating in. This will also help you to identify those families who might need that additional support (financial, clothing or ideas).

Often children will discover an activity outside of school that they can excel at or achieve success, and this can be important to the development of their self-esteem and confidence especially if they are struggling with some aspects of the curriculum.

Physical skills movement and learning

The section on movement and learning emphasised the importance of providing regular opportunities for children to practise basic foundational skills such as running, jumping, throwing, catching and kicking a ball and balancing. School holidays, particularly the longer Easter and summer holidays provide an opportunity for parents to encourage their children to build their physical skills.

- Consider compiling a list of ideas and activities for parents to follow at home that are affordable or free.
- There could be a news flash on the school website, Facebook page or newsletter that goes out to parents just before the school holidays reminding parents about local activities that are available. Many local councils have a directory of leisure and community activities available on their websites.
- Create a link to the NHS 'Change for life' programme that has ideas for parents to involve their children in physical activities, alongside healthy eating tips and recipes. www.nhs.uk/change4life/

The Forest School (www.forestschoolassociation.org) curriculum has opened opportunities for outdoor play and learning experiences to be available for all children. Sharing ideas children have participated in at Forest School can help parents and children appreciate that going outside in all weathers can be fun and help build confidence in physical skills.

Learning to ride a bike

Learning to ride a bike is an important life skill for young children, enabling them to explore their environment, play with other children and keep healthy. Cycling can be a difficult skill for children to master involving as it does good coordination, strength and balance. Parents may need guidance about how to get started – Early Years and school settings can promote the benefits of cycling to parents, and many schools operate a cycle to school scheme in years 5–7. Some settings will host *Bikeability* training utilising school playgrounds as a safe place to practise balance and pedal skills (Department of Transport, https://bikeability.org.uk/bikeability-training/).

Bikeability level one requires children to be able to pedal and glide before commencing the training. Young children can be encouraged to build basic bike skills at home in the following ways:

- A balance bike familiarises young children with the balance required and sensation of riding a proper bike, it can encourage coordination of the arms and legs working together that's needed to propel forwards.
- Scooters are also a great way to encourage young children to balance and steer. Three-wheeled scooters provide more stability for children who might find balance and coordination difficult.
- Encouraging the habit of donning a helmet when using a balance bike or scooter. Encourage the child to put on the helmet independently and fasten the strap. Start with a long strap and then tighten.

- Ensure the child understands how to operate the brakes on a bike and the back stop on a scooter before setting off.
- Practise getting on and off the bike and scooter before pushing forwards and then practise stopping and starting again.
- Encourage the child to look forwards and to be aware of others and their environment.
- Start scooting in a straight line before introducing obstacles to navigate and steer around.
- Practise lots and lots of times and have fun.

Swimming

Learning to swim is an important survival skill, but it is also a great way for children to have fun with their friends and family and a good way to keep fit. Learning to swim as a child can encourage a lifelong habit with long-term health and wellbeing benefits. It is a great way to build confidence and self-esteem. By the age of four most children are ready to learn to swim. Advice about where to find lessons and how parents can teach their children basic swimming skills can be found at *Swim England*, the national governing board for swimming in England (www.swimming.org/learntoswim/learn-to-swim-information-for-parents/getting-started/).

Independent skills

Mealtimes at home

Many families no longer routinely sit down together every day to eat a meal at home and this may explain why so many children struggle with the skills associated with eating a meal when they start Early Years – for example using different eating utensils and learning to pour a drink. Many families will eat 'on the go' or children eat alone in front of the television. Encourage families to have a least one meal a week together for the following reasons:

- Children love to be asked to set the table – where they learn about eating utensils, but also about left and right and where they can develop the coordination skills needed to place and fold napkins.
- Let the child contribute to and help in the preparation of the food, such as preparing fruit for a fruit salad or washing salad.
- Remember to provide suitable seating for children and encourage 'good' sitting (feet on a firm surface, elbows at table height).
- Demonstrate how to cut up their food and use a knife and fork or other eating utensils.
- Children learn by watching and imitating, encourage the basic rules of sharing a meal, not eating with your mouth open etc. Encourage simple 'please' and 'thank you' when asking for things.

Working together with parents and carers

Getting ready for school

Home is where most children will learn how to dress themselves. Learning to put on their school clothes helps a child's confidence and their developing coordination skills. Below is some general advice for parents when children are struggling with getting ready for school.

- The most important thing is to give children sufficient time when they are learning to dress – remember mastering skills such as fastening buttons takes a long time and requires lots of practise.
- When short of time ask the child to do the easy tasks themselves (push feet into shoes) while you do the difficult parts (fasten buckle).
- Always give lots of praise and rewards.
- Choose weekends or holiday times when there is more time to practise the more difficult dressing skills such as learning how to zip up a coat or tie shoelaces.
- Play dressing up games and have a dressing up box where children can have fun and experiment with different fastenings and clothing.
- Choose school wear that is easy for the child to get on and off and opt for slightly looser underwear, clothes and socks.
- Choose elasticated trousers and skirts and loose tops. Choose shoes with Velcro fastening or slip on shoes.

Getting clothes back to front and inside out and mixing up left and right are common problems for young children – here are some ideas to help:

- Choose clothes that have a clear front and back, ask children to find the label at the back or locate the design of the school logo on their pullover to help orientate front and back.
- Demonstrate how to turn a jumper right side out. Draw their attention to seams and differences in shade and texture between front and insides.
- Mark shoes left and right on the inside.

There is lots of practical advice and support for parents about dressing and other independence skills on the Australian parent website https://raisingchildren.net.au/toddlers/health-daily-care/dressing/how-to-get-dressed.

Going to the loo

Most children will be toilet trained on starting Early Years but not all. Some children although able to use the toilet independently may continue to have problems with bed wetting, constipation or other problems. Wiping is often a significant problem for young children. Early Years practitioners can signpost parents and families to advice and support at The Children's Bowel and Bladder Charity ERIC www.eric.org.uk.

Working together

So far in this section we have talked about how you as professionals and practitioners can provide parents and carers with ideas about how to support the development of their children's motor and coordination skills, and thus benefiting their academic achievement as well. However, there are lots of things that can be practiced and supported either by practitioners alone, or together with parents and carers, within settings.

Hopefully, you will have noticed as you have read through each section of the book that there are the odd sentences written in blue? We did this to show you that everything discussed in this book can and should involve and include parents and carers. Parents and carers are the 'golden thread' and need to be actively engaged with in all aspects of their child's development and learning. I expect there are many exciting things you already do that enable you to build and develop positive and fruitful relationships with your parents. It is however good to regularly reflect on how and when you do this and whether all parents and carers can participate in the joint working activities you offer and provide.

Try this

Read through the table called 'Working Together' (Table 5. 1) which outlines the opportunities to work with parents and carers. Then go through your weekly plans and see where parents could be involved in playing with/visiting or participating in some joint activities. Have a display which gives positive encouragement to parents/carers to participate in nursery/school life as much as they can ... even on an online forum or through sharing pictures their child has made. This latter point is now vital as so many parents and carers have little choice about whether and when they work.

Think about this

Table 5.1 'Working Together' draws together all the suggestions and comments made about working with parents and carers throughout the book. Take a look at these and think whether you already offer something similar or not and whether all children and parents and carers are able to join in. Of course, shift work and working away from home will mean that not everyone can attend everything, but there does need to be the opportunity for the main outside the home worker to participate in one or two activities each year. Think of the smiles that you see on the children's faces when family members arrive to see them perform or share in an exciting adventure (e.g. a bear hunt). This must tell us something very important and we believe that working together benefits everyone, but of course, mostly the children.

Working together with parents and carers

Table 5.1 Working Together

Book chapter	Comments in section	Further suggestions
1	Involve families and parents so that the child can be encouraged to practise skills at home and during holidays. Remember you might also want to include parents in this decision making. Changing for PE may also be an important outcome for parents, who would really appreciate their child being able to do up their own clothes in a busy household. Encourage parents to practise catching and throwing at home.	Provide parents with information about where they can take their children during the holidays (free or low charge). Ask parents if there is any information e.g. about the latest games played in nursery, they would like to have for the holidays. Provide each parent with a visual schedule of how their child can learn to dress / undress themselves. This can be differentiated depending on the needs of the child. Obviously outside in the garden, park, countryside or beach is easiest, but if space is limited practising with a soft ball or balloon inside the home can help children develop the coordination skills needed.
2	Don't forget to encourage parents to buy clothes for their children that have large buttons and button holes. In this way practise can take place at nursery or school and home. Ensure that children have clothing that is appropriate and fits them. It is easier to take off and put on clothing that is loose. Tight fitting pants and tops are harder to get on and off. Involve the child's parents in setting realistic targets and encourage practice at home as well as school. Involving parents and families is a great way to help children make progress in personal independence skills. Why not invite parents to join in with a session you have planned? Give families activities that they can do at home and tell them why it is important for their child to be able to gain these skills. Parents don't need to do formal 'exercises' with their children, but regular practise at the weekend or on holiday can help a child develop. For many children it will be the first time that they will use a toilet away from home. A small number of children may have a medical condition or difficulty that affects their bladder and bowel and ability to use the toilet. If this is the case it is important to involve the family and multidisciplinary team in determining how to manage the child's personal hygiene needs. Early intervention and collaboration between Early Years settings and home can help establish the routines to support toilet training.	With a uniform / most comfortable clothing for nursery/ school you send home add a note about trying to buy loose fitting clothes with large buttons and button holes. Ask parents to help you with this. Ask parents what they would like their child to be able to do next and how much help / time they think they will need to achieve this. How many times each year do you invite parents into the nursery to play and have fun with their child? Ensure that anything you ask to be completed at home can be achieved in a fun way. Try and collect information about individual children as soon as possible, making sure parents know they will still have a place at your nursery / school, even if their child has difficulties with their bladder or bowel.
3	Don't forget to share this sitting song with parents and carers so that they can think about where and how their child sits to colour, draw and read. Share this information (stability) with parents and carers so that they can also support their child's development.v	Perhaps this song can be sung to parents at an assembly or end of term 'show'. Then a sheet or recording can be sent home to help parents learn the words! This is important because children love making things at home. If parents know about the importance of good supportive seating and an appropriate sized table they will try their best to provide it even if it means going down to the library or local children's centre / club.

(Continued)

Book chapter	Comments in section	Further suggestions
4	Involve parents and carers by inviting children to take into nursery / school examples of drawing and writing from home, and send home examples of their school work.	This exchange of positive examples of work needs to be a celebration of working together and must provide children with a visible positive image of parents working together with professionals.
	Engage with parents and carers about their thoughts on handwriting styles.	
	Think about possible training needs of staff and parents (and the budget required to do this).	As you will have read, handwriting styles is a 'contested' area and one which parents and the nursery / school will have a view on. As a nursery / school it would be helpful to explain your reasons for making the decisions you do about handwriting. Parents are then fully briefed and will most likely be more generally accepting of the nursery /school's approach.
	Parental involvement is also extremely valuable in supporting handwriting. Over half the children who have accessed the fine motor skills interventions to date were also found to have difficulties with self-care skills involving their hands, such as managing zips and buttons and eating with a knife and fork. Therefore, it is important that parents are also encouraged to practise life skills on a daily basis at home.	This applies equally to the training of staff and they of course should be fully involved with making / adjusting their practice.
	Don't forget to involve the child's parents in all these discussions because they can help by continuing to practise fun activities at home with the child.	Put up posters / children's work completing tasks such as eating with a knife and fork or doing up zips. Why not have a large zip on display so that parents can be encouraged to let their child 'have a go'.
		A parent forum (this does not have to be a physical forum) sharing ideas about how to help children with self-care skills can be a helpful idea.

Summary

Understanding the importance of the development of coordination and movement skills for academic learning is not just for those children with additional needs or disabilities but for every child. It is not an 'additional' part of education but an essential key element and needs to be prioritised especially within an Early Years curriculum.

As this book has demonstrated, early motor and coordination skills are crucial for many aspects of a young child's life and the gaining of many self-care and functional skills. They also can impact on a child's self-esteem, friendships and academic engagement.

If these skills can have such an impact at this stage of life, imagine how detrimental it might be for those young people with continuing issues as they enter adolescence and adult life. The importance of the role Early Years education, practitioners and teachers play in providing the nurturing and supportive environment children need to develop personal life skills can therefore not be overstated (Buttle UK 2019).

References

Abbott, R., Straker, L., and Mathiassen, S. (2013) "Patterning of children's sedentary time at and away from school." *Obesity*, 21 (1): 2012–2014.

Baines, E., and Blatchford, P. (2019). *School Break and Lunchtimes and Young People's Social Lives: A Follow Up Study*. Nuffield Foundation. Available at: www.breaktime.org.uk/Publications/Baines%2042402%20BreaktimeSurvey%20-%20Main%20public%20report%20(May19)-Final.pdf.

Blythe, S. (2015) *Boosting Learning in the Primary Classroom*. Abingdon: David Fulton.

Brian, A. and Taunton, S. (2018) "Effectiveness of motor skill intervention varies based on implementation strategy." *Physical Education and Sport Pedagogy*, 23 (2): 222–233. doi:10.1080/17408989.2017.1413709.

Brown, C.G. (2010) "Improving fine motor skills in young children: an intervention study". *Educational Psychology in Practice*, *26*, (3), September 2010: 269–278.

Bruns, D. and Thompson, S. (2014) "Turning mealtimes into learning opportunities." *Teaching Exceptional Children*, 46 (6): 179–186.

Buttle UK. (2019) "Chances for children – what is it like for children growing up in the UK." Available at: www.buttleuk.org/news/child-poverty-in-uk-in-2019. http://s3-eu-west-1.amazonaws.com/files.buttle.org.uk/State_of_Child_Poverty_Report_July_2019.pdf.

Children's food trust. (2013) *Good Food for Small Schools – A Practical Toolkit*. Available at: www.schoolfoodplan.com/wp-content/uploads/2016/03/CFT-SmallSchoolToolkit.pdf.

Cleaton, M. A. M., Lorgelly, P. K., & Kirby, A. (2020). Developmental coordination disorder in UK children aged 6–18 years: Estimating the cost. *British Journal of Occupational Therapy*, *83*(1), 29–40. doi:https://doi.org/10.1177/0308022619866642

Connell, G., and McCarthy, C. (2013) *A Moving Child Is a Learning Child*. Minneapolis, MN: Free Spirit Publishing. ISBN-10: 1575424355.

Cripps, C. (1995). *A Hand for Spelling 2a*. Wisbech: LDA.

Dawson D. R., McEwen S. E., Polatajko H. J. (2017) *Cognitive orientation to daily occupational performance in occupational therapy – using the CO-OP Approach™ to enable participation across lifespan*. Bethesda, MD: AOTA Press.

Department for Education. (2015) *Advice on Standards for School Premises*. Available at: https://assets.publishing.service.gov.uk/government/uploads/system/uploads/attachment_data/file/410294/Advice_on_standards_for_school_premises.pdf.

Department for Work and Pensions. (2019). *Households below Average Income, Statistics on the Number and Percentage of People Living in Low Income Households for Financial Years 1994/95 to 2017/18*. Available at: www.gov.uk/government/statistics/households-below-average-income-199495-to-201718.

Dimbleby, H. and Vincent, J. (2014) *The School Food Plan*. Available at: www.schoolfoodplan.com.

Eddy, L., Wood, M., Shire, K., Bingham, D., Bonnick, E., Creaser, A., Mon-Williams, M., and Hill, L. (2019) "A systematic review of randomised and case-controlled trials investigating the effectiveness of school-based motor-skill interventions in 3–12 year old children." *Child Care Health and Development*. doi:10.1111/cch.12712.

Education and Resources for Improving Childhood Continence (ERIC). (2006) *Water is Cool in School*. Available at: http://complexneeds.org.uk/modules/Module-4.2-Safeguarding---privacy,-dignity-and-personal-care/All/downloads/m14p090b/wicis_booklet.pdf.

Education and Resources for Improving Childhood Continence (ERIC). (2017) *Thinking about Wee and Poo Now You're on Your Way to School. Children's Bowel and Bladder Charity*. Available at: www.eric.org.uk/Handlers/Download.ashx?IDMF=dc253d91-a28b-47ef-a288-92cebb0add76.

Education and Resources for Improving Childhood Continence (ERIC). (2019) *'The Right to Go' – School Toilet Charter. Children's Bowel and Bladder Charity*. Available at: www.eric.org.uk/Handlers/Download.ashx?IDMF=ad817276-bb45-49c9-b430-ad6e4d220b5a.

Fedewa, A. L. and Ahn, S. (2011) "The effects of physical activity and physical fitness on children's achievement and cognitive outcomes." *Research Quarterly for Exercise and Sport*, 82 (3): 521–535. doi:10.1080/02701367.2011.10599785.

Graham, P., Russo, R., and Defeyter, M. (2015) "The advantages and disadvantages of breakfast clubs according to parents, children, and school staff in the North East of England, UK." *Frontiers in Public Health*, 3: 156.

Harrowell, I., Hollen, L., Lingam, R., & Emond, A. (2018). The impact of developmental coordination disorder on educational achievement in secondary school. *Research in Developmental Disabilities*, 72, 13–22. doi:https://doi.org/10.1016/j.ridd.2017.10.014.

Hayton, J., Wall, K., and Dimitriou, D. (2018) "Get your coat: examining the development of independent dressing skills in young children with visual impairment, Down syndrome and typically developing children." *International Journal of Inclusive Education*, 1–16. doi:10.1080/13603116.2018.1456568.

Howard, J. (2017) *Mary D Sheridan's Play in Early Childhood: From Birth to Six Years*. Abingdon: Routledge.

Howe, T. and Oldham, J. (2010) "Posture and balance." In Trew, M., and Kell, C. (Eds.) *Human Movement an Introductory Text*. 6th ed. London: Churchill Livingstone.

Howells, K. and Sääkslahti, A. (2019) "Physical activity recommendations for early childhood: an international analysis of ten different countries' current national physical activity policies and practices for those under the age of 5." In UNSPECIFIED (Ed.) *Physical Education in Early Childhood Education and Care. Researches – Best Practices – Situation*. 1st ed. Bratislava: Federation Internationale D'Education Physique, pp. 321–336. ISBN 978-80-89075-81-2.

Hoy, M. M. P., Egan, M. Y., and Feder, K. P. (2011) "A systematic review of interventions to improve handwriting." *Canadian Journal of Occupational Therapy*, 78: 13–25. doi:10.2182/cjot.2011.78.1.3.

Hulme P. (undated) https://nha-handwriting.org.uk/handwriting/articles/teaching-fully-cursive-writing-in-reception/.

Hutton, E. (2009a) "Beginning to sparkle." *Early Years Educator*, 11 (7) November 2009: v–vii.

Hutton, E. (2009b) "Occupational therapy in mainstream primary schools: an evaluation of a pilot project." *British Journal of Occupational Therapy*, 72 (7): 308–313.

Hutton, E. and Soan, S. (2010) "Skills for primary schools: movement and coordination resources." *Support for Learning*, 25 (3): 116–121.

Hutton, E., Tuppeney, S., and Hasselbusch, A. (2016) "Making the case for universal and targeted children's occupational therapy in the United Kingdom." *British Journal of Occupational Therapy*, 79 (7): 450–453.

References

Hutton, H. and Soan, S. (2015) "'Lessons learned' from introducing universal strategies designed to support the motor and functional skills of reception and year 1 children in a sample of primary schools in South East England." *Education 3–13: International Journal of Primary, Elementary and Early Years Education*. doi:10.1080/03004279.2015.1048270.

Jones, B. (2018) "Making time for family meals: parental influences, home eating environments, barriers and protective factors." *Physiology & Behavior*, 193: 248–251.

Joseph Rowntree Foundation. (2018) *Destitution in the UK*. Available at: www.jrf.org.uk/report/destitution-uk-2018.

Kehily, J. (Ed.) (2013) *Understanding Childhood: A Cross-Disciplinary Approach*. Bristol: The Policy Press, pp. 53–98.

Lewis, A. (2019) "Examining the concept of well-being and early childhood: adopting multi-disciplinary perspectives." *Journal of Early Childhood Research*. doi:10.1177/1476718X19860553.

MacArthur, C. A., Graham, S., and Fitzgerald, J. (2006) *Handbook of Writing Research*. London: Guildford Press.

Mavilidi, M. F., Okely, A. D., Chandler, P., and Paas, F. (2016) "Infusing physical activities into the classroom: effects on preschool children's geography learning." *Mind Brain Education*, 10 (4): 256–263. doi:10.1111/mbe.12131.

McMurray, S., Drysdale, J., and Jordan, G. (2009) "Motor processing difficulties: guidance for teachers in mainstream classrooms." *Support for Learning*, 24 (3) August 2009: 119–125.

Missiuna, C., Pollock, N., Campbell, W., DeCola, C., Hecimovich, C., Sahagian Whalen, S., Siemon, J., Song, K., Gaines, R., Bennett, S., McCauley, D., Stewart, D., Cairney, J., Dix, L., and Camden, C. (2017) "Using an innovative model of service delivery to identify children who are struggling in school." *British Journal of Occupational Therapy*, 80 (3): 145–154. doi:10.1177/0308022616679852.

Mitchell, J. and Byun, W. (2014) "Sedentary behavior and health outcomes in children and adolescents." *American Journal of Lifestyle Medicine*, 8 (3): 173–199. Available at: http://ajl.sagepub.com/content/8/3/173.

Montgomery, D. (2007) *Spelling, Handwriting and Dyslexia*. London and New York: Routledge.

Mullender-Wijnsma, M. J., Hartman, E., de Greeff, J. W., Bosker, R. J., Doolaard, S., and Visscher, C. (2015) "Improving academic performance of school-age children by physical activity in the classroom: 1 year program evaluation." *Journal of School Heath*, 85: 365–371. Available at: www.ltl.org.uk/wp-content/uploads/2019/02/improving-academic-performance-of-school-age-children.pdf.

National Health Service. (2020) "Change 4 life, 10 minute shake up games." Available at: www.nhs.uk/10-minute-shake-up/shake-ups?filter=frozen#shakeups-hub.

Ofsted. (2019) *The Education Inspection Framework*. Available at: https://assets.publishing.service.gov.uk/government/uploads/system/uploads/attachment_data/file/801429/Education_inspection_framework.pdf.

Patton, S. and Hutton, E. (2017) "Exploring the participation of children with Down Syndrome in Handwriting Without Tears." *Journal of Occupational Therapy, Schools, & Early Intervention*, 10(2), pp. 171–184. doi: 10.1080/19411243.2017.1292485.

Pedro, A., Goldschmidt, T., and Daniels, L. (2019) "Parent carer awareness and understanding of dyspraxia: implications for child development support practices." *Journal of Psychology in Africa*, 29 (1): 87–91. doi:10.1080/14330237.2019.1568092.

Prado, E. and Dewey, K. (2014) "Nutrition and brain development in early life." *Nutrition Reviews*, 72 (4): 267–284. doi:10.1111/nure.12102.

Rhemtulla, M. and Tucker-Drob, E. M. (2011) "Correlated longitudinal changes across linguistic, achievement, and psychomotor domains in early childhood: evidence for a global dimension of development." *Developmental Science*, *14*(5), 2011: 1245–1254.

Routen, A., Johnston, J., Glazebrook, C., and Sherar, L. (2018). "Teacher perceptions on the delivery and implementation of movement integration strategies." *The CLASS PAL (Physically Active Learning) Programme*, 88, March 2018: 48–58. doi:10.1016/j.ijer.2018.01.003.

Schneck, C. M. and Amundson, S. J. (2010) "Prewriting and handwriting skills." In Case-Smith, J. and O'Brien, J. C. (Eds.) *Occupational Therapy for Children*. 6th ed. St. Louis, MO: Mosby/Elsevier, pp. 555–580.

Seifert, A. and Metz, A. (2017) "The effects of inflated seating cushions on engagement in preschool circle time." *Early Childhood Education Journal*, 45 (3): 411–418. doi:10.1007/s10643-016-0797-7.

Sharma, A. and Cockerill, H. (2014) *From Birth to Five Years: Children's Developmental Progress*. Abingdon: Routledge.

Steele, H., Bate, J., Steele, M., Dube, S. R., Danskin, K., Knafo, H., Nikitiades, A., Bonuck, K., Meissner, P. and Murphy, A. (2016) "Adverse Childhood Experiences, Poverty, and Parenting Stress." *Canadian Journal of Behavioural Science / Revue canadienne des sciences du comportement*, 48(1): 32–38.

Strauss, D. (undated) *Don't Stop the Song and Dance: An Evaluation of Write Dance Practices in Schools and Early Years Settings*. Canterbury Christ Church University.

Sugden, D. and Wade, M. (2013) *Typical and Atypical Motor Development*. London: Mac Keith Press.

The Children's Society. (2019) *Good Childhood Report*. Available at: www.childrenssociety.org.uk/sites/default/files/the_good_childhood_report_2019_summary.pdf.

The Marmot Review. (2010) "Fair society, healthy lives." *The Health Foundation*. Available at: www.local.gov.uk/marmot-review-report-fair-society-healthy-lives.

Tomporowski, P., MuCullick, B., and Pesce, C. (2015) "Enhancing children's cognition with physical activity games." In P. Tomporowski, B. MuCullick and C. Pesce (Eds.) *Human Kinetics*. Mitcham: Human Kinetics Australia. ISBN 9781450441421.

United Kingdom, Chief Medical Officer. (2019) "Physical activity guidelines." Available at: https://assets.publishing.service.gov.uk/government/uploads/system/uploads/attachment_data/file/829882/1-physical-activity-for-early-years-birth-to-5.pdf.

Webb, A. (undated) "Continuous cursive: Cure or curse?" *National Handwriting Association*. Available at: https://nha-handwriting.org.uk/handwriting/articles/continuous-cursive-cure-or-curse/.

Wickramasinghe, K., Rayner, M., Goldacre, M., Townsend, N., and Scarborough, P. (2017) "Environmental and nutrition impact of achieving new School Food Plan recommendations in the primary school meals sector in England." *BMJ Open*, 7: e013840. doi:10.1136/bmjopen-2016-013840.

Wolpert, D. M., Ghahramani, Z., and Flanagan, J. R. (2001) "Perspectives and problems in motor learning." *Trends in Cognitive Sciences*, 5: 487–494.

World Health Organization. (2019) "Guidelines on physical activity, sedentary behaviour and sleep for children under 5 years of age." Geneva ISBN 978-92-

4-155053-6. Available at: www.who.int/publications-detail/guidelines-on-physical-activity-sedentary-behaviour-and-sleep-for-children-under-5-years-of-age.

Zwicker, J. and Harris, S. (2009) "A reflection on motor learning theory in pediatric occupational therapy practice." *Canadian Journal of Occupational Therapy*, 76: 29–37.

Resources

Box of Ideas. Available at: www.boxofideas.org/ideas/practical-skills-in-education/pre-school/toileting-for-school/.

Bikeability programme (Department of Transport). Available at: https://bikeability.org.uk/bikeability-training/.

Education and Resources for Improving Childhood Continence (ERIC) (Education and Information for Improving Child Continence). Available at: www.eric.org.uk.

National Handwriting Association. Available at: https://nha-handwriting.org.uk/handwriting/articles/teaching-fully-cursive-writing-in-reception/.

NHS 'Change for Life' programme. Available at: www.nhs.uk/change4life/.

Parental support for independence skills. Available at: https://raisingchildren.net.au/toddlers/health-daily-care/dressing/how-to-get-dressed.

Penpals for Handwriting. Available at: www.cambridge.org/penpals.

Swim England. Available at: www.swimming.org/learntoswim/learn-to-swim-information-for-parents/getting-started/.

The Children's Bowel and Bladder Charity ERIC. Available at: www.eric.org.uk.

Index

Abbott, R. 41
Amundson, S. J. 13, 36

Baines, E. 18
balancing 9–10, 26, 30–31; and riding a bike 62–63
base of support 10
bilateral task 26
bladder 30–31, 64
Blatchford, P. 18
Blythe, S. 44, 46
body awareness *see* movement
bowel 30–31, 64
Brian, A. 14
Brown, C. E. 1
Bruns, D. 18
Buttle UK 8, 67
buttons *see* dressing
Byun, W. 41

catching 10
chewing 23–24; and swallowing 23–24
classroom design and learning 40–41
Cleaton, M. A. M. 1
Cockerill, H. 7, 8, 13, 25
colouring 49–50
Connell, G. 13
continence 30
coordination 26; skills 27, 38
Cripps, C. 54
cursive script *see* handwriting
cutlery 20–23

Dawson, D. R. 12
Department for Education 31, 54
Department for Work and Pensions 61
developmental coordination disorder 29–30
Dewey, K. 18
Dimbleby, H. 20
Down syndrome 30
Dressing 24, 64; and buttons 26; changing for PE 27–28; and zips 27
dyspraxia *see* developmental coordination disorder

eating 18–19
Eddy, L. 14

Fedewa, A. L. 5
food poverty 18–19
furniture: chairs and desks 35–36; dining room 19–20

Graham, P. 18

handwriting: case study 58–59; complex task 44–45; cursive script 55; developmental skills 45–46; difficulties 59–60; individual letters 54; and learning to write 47; and left-handed writer 52–53; and motor and sensory skills 46; policy 56–57; and in school 44; and teaching 54
Harris, S. 55
Harrowell, I. 1
Hayton, J. 30
Howard, J. 141
Howe, T. 5, 35
Howells, K. 5
Hoy, M. M. P. 55
Hulme, P. 54
Hutton, E. xiii, 30

individual letters *see* handwriting

Jones, B. 18
Joseph Rowntree Foundation 18
jumping 11

Kehily, J. vii

left-handed writer *see* handwriting
Lewis, A. vii
lunchtime 17–18; dining area 19–20; furniture 22; importance of 18; observation checklist 21; skills 21

MacArthur, C. A. 54
mark-making: to writing 50; environment 50–51

Index

Mathiassen, S. 41
Mavilidi, M. F. 6
McCarthy, C. 13
McMurray, S. 60
Metz, A. 39
Missiuna, C. 30
Mitchell, J. 41
Montgomery, D. 55
motor skills 7, 27; fine 47; gross 46–47; problem 1
move: and interact 13; observation checklist 14–15
movement: and coordination 1; core 8; environment 12–13; gross 13; and learning 12–13; precision skills 13, 26, 38; and skills 7–8
Mullender-Wijnsma, M. J. 6
multidisciplinary vii; team 13, 16, 30
muscle tone 42

National Curriculum 55
National Health Service (NHS) 6
nutrition 18

occupational therapists 30
Ofsted 19
Oldham, J. 35

parents 12, 16, 25, 26, 30, 51, 57, 59, 60
parent governors 61
Patton, S. 30
Pedro, A. vii
pencil grips 48; cylindrical 48; difficulties 49; digital 48; left- handed writers 52; modified tripod grip 48; tripod 49
perception 26; skills 26
physical activity 5, 62
physical education (PE) see dressing
postural: support 22; control 34–35
posture 34; stability 36
Prado, E. 18
precision skills see movements (fine)
proprioception 29

readiness for school 64
Rhemtulla, M. 1

riding a bike 62–63
Routen, A. 39

Sääkslahti, A. 5
Schneck, C. M. 13, 36
school meals 18
seating: plan 38; position 52
Siefert, A. 39
self-esteem 59
sensory awareness 13
sense of: balance 13; self 13; touch 13; understanding 26
Sharma, A. 7, 8, 13, 25
sitting: comfortably 35–37; cross-legged 38–39; difficulties 41; and learning 37–41
Soan, S. xiii, 7
stability 13; core 42
Straker, L. 41
Strauss, D. 47
Sugden, D. 13, 14
swimming 63

Taunton, S. 14
The Children's Society see food poverty
The Marmot Review (2010) vii
Thompson, S. 18
toileting 30; bottom cleaning/wiping skills 33, 64; skills 31–33; use of 30–31

United Kingdom, Chief Medical Officer 6, 35
universal provision 1

Vincent, J. 20
visual skills 47
visual tracking 26

Wade, M. 13, 14
Webb, A. 54
Wickramasinghe, K. 18
Wolpert, D. M. 7
World Health Organisation (WHO) 5–7

zips see dressing
Zwicker, J. 55